ONE AMONG MAN₁

The story of Sunderland Rugby Football Club
(1873-date) in its historical context

By

Keith Gregson

Paperback ISBN 978-1-907685-99-6
ePub ISBN 978-1-907685-17-0
Mobipocket ISBN 978-1-907685-18-7
Published in the UK by MX Publishing
335 Princess Park Manor, Royal Drive, London, N11 3GX
www.mx-publishing.co.uk [UK]
www.mxpublishing.com [USA]

Cover Artwork by www.staunch.com

This book is dedicated to all Sunderland RFC players who are no longer with us and, in particular, to Ian Herbert (1965 –2010) who was helping with research into the club's history at the time of his sudden death. He epitomises the spirit of the club.

'Herbie was a tough character on the pitch and a gentleman off it. He was one who would always play hard and would never give up regardless of the score; he always gave his all for the cause. Asked by a number of other clubs to go and play for them, he wasn't interested. He was 'Ashbrooke' through and through.'

Jim Smith (former 1st XV captain) December 2010

Unknown Sunderland RFC player (c.1886)

'There is a fellowship about it that makes it the envy of most other games.'

Sir William Ramsay, President of the Rugby Football Union, 1971

Table of Contents

Foreword - Sunderland RFC - A Proud Heritage

'One Among Many' may not seem a particularly inviting title for a book so it is a choice that needs some explanation.

Sunderland Rugby Football Club, founded in 1873, could well be described as 'one among many' in the early twenty-first century. It is not among the big boys in a national or even regional Rugby Union league. Rather it is one of some 60% of the clubs that plays mainly for pleasure, week in week out, at a local level. Yet this is only part of the story. The club has an interesting history which can be told thanks to the survival of the records of the wider Ashbrooke Sports Club, of which the rugby club is a part. The sports club itself, founded in 1887 as the Sunderland Cricket and Football Club, is a rare survival from Victorian times and also an important element in the rugby club's tale.

THE SUNDERLAND CRICKET & FOOTBALL CLUB.

Heading from an 1895 audit

Sunderland Rugby Football Club (RFC) has been on the go for almost one hundred and forty years. The letters RFC behind the club name tell the tale; quite simply, the club was formed some years before 'union' and 'league' separated in the 1890s, causing clubs starting thereafter to be designated RUFC and RLFC. In fact the Ashbrooke archives show Sunderland's rugby club to have been known as Sunderland Football Club (FC) both before and after the internationally famous Sunderland Association Football Club (AFC) came into being in 1879. In the late Victorian and early Edwardian periods, Sunderland

RFC was one of the most significant clubs in the north of England. The 1st XV won the first ever Durham County Cup and a wonderful hand-tinted photograph of the side clearly shows one team member sporting an England cap (see frontispiece). In the first decade of the twentieth century, the club was among the strongest in the region with its players providing the backbone for a hugely successful Durham County side.

Between the wars, the club enjoyed a couple of successful County Cup runs and also saw the appearance in its ranks of three players - Eric Watt Moses, Alan Bean and Hartley Elliott - all of whom were later to put their stamp on both the national and international game.

The history of Sunderland RFC up to the early 1960s has been well chronicled and notes a number of sad losses in wartime and another memorable County Cup success in the late 1950s. More recently, the club has been affected by the introduction of leagues and professionalism into the game and by the huge growth in mini and junior rugby.

In 2011, Sunderland RFC remains a friendly and sociable club and part of a much wider Ashbrooke setup which embraces the bowls, tennis, hockey, rugby and cricket clubs of the city of Sunderland. Over the years Ashbrooke has had image problems, frequently rooted in the club's origins among the upper middle classes and former public schoolboys of the then town. These are now in the past and, in the professional era, the rugby club continues to acknowledge many of the qualities which make the sport a hobby to be enjoyed by all.

Unique in some senses, the history of Sunderland RFC cannot be allowed to stand alone. As a practising social historian, I firmly believe that a social history of our country must cover every aspect of life, including sport, and that the full story of English social life is ultimately a sum of its parts. Rugby football has affected the lives of many people. As former England captain Richard Hill notes in another MX publication, based upon Clifton RFC, "rugby clubs provide a vital role in their community". Hopefully this book and some of its content will encourage others to examine the story of their own club 'in a historical context'.

Returning to the subject of 'one among many', there is a further twist in the tale. Not only is Sunderland RFC a rugby club, it is one among many as a single sports section of the wider Ashbrooke Sports Club. The relationship between rugby club and sports club is an important and intriguing one and, though its story is told separately (in Appendix One) it is key to the main tale. The same can be said about the separate biographies of chosen club figures (Appendix Two). The final appendix (Appendix Three) deals with a side topic that raised its head during the research process. Clearly a number of those who played rugby for Sunderland RFC over the years had both the time and the ability to excel at other sports - a subject worthy of study and comment.

It is hoped that what follows will be of interest and of use to many different readers. Those with a connection to the club past and present will be able to pick out well-known names and events although, arguably, they may have wished for a little more solid detail. That has been sacrificed so that the book can be of interest to non-Sunderland folk with a passion for the history of sport. The professional sports historian, however, may have liked a little more in the way of sourcing and cross-referencing. These points are being made now, simply to avoid criticism later!

Many people have made this work possible, including some that are no longer with us. Over the years men such as Eric Watt Moses, Alan Bean and Hartley Elliott have kept their eye on archival material - also others who have contributed to the thorough 1960s history of the wider sports club, in *To Ashbrooke and Beyond*.

In more recent years Robin Auld and John Buddington have shown a real interest in the club's history. The modern officials and staff, especially Rob Deverson, Paul Amundsen and Gerard Harvey have been helpful and encouraging, as have staff at the City Centre Local Studies Centre and the Sunderland Museum and Winter Gardens. Steve Emecx at MX Publishing has also taken the risk of publishing a book, after he had it described to him in a mere hundred words. Club members have lent a hand in their numbers, with special thanks going out to Paul Sturgess, Jim Smith, Kev Logan, Tommy Harrison, Steve Harrison, Jamie Boyd, Andy Kyle and Rob Stormont for their assistance and observations. Friend and award-winning sports historian, Mike Huggins, has also offered advice although I am certain that what follows will fail to match the quality of his own published work. Also thanks to proofreader Jack Deverson of *JD Editorial Services*, a talented all-round sportsman himself at 18 (rowing, cricket and bowls but sadly not rugby). Jack has given his professional services freely.

Above all, my thanks go to my family who brought me to Ashbrooke in the first place - to my wife Barbara, for a number of years redoubtable 'shirt lady' of the mini and junior section - and to our three sons Tom, John and Paul - all of whom still enjoy their sport today.

Thanks to the generosity of the publishers, much of the profit from this book will go to the rugby club. Readers will soon work out where it will be spent, viz., on those things that an annual 'hand to mouth' existence has so far placed beyond the power of the club's purse.

Keith Gregson B.A. M.Litt (Ashbrooke archivist)

Footnote

Money rears its ugly head from time to time in the book. Up to the 1970s, it is often given in pounds, shillings and pence and some effort has been made to relate the sum to decimal currency. Unfortunately there isn't the space to go into detail about the relative value of money so sums which will today appear small may have been quite large at the time. Here, the advice is to go on to one of the online comparative sites where wages and expenditure past and present are compared.

The spelling of Holmeside/Holmside, one of the club's early grounds, is disputed. I have used the modern spelling with the 'e'.

About the author

Keith Gregson (b. 1948) is a writer, historian and musician who was in charge of history teaching at a large urban comprehensive school for over thirty years. He was Burn Prize historian at the University of Newcastle in 1970 and has a Masters Degree in English Social History. He has been involved in sport at Ashbrooke since the 1970s and has written about the wider club's history for over thirty years. Keith was in charge of mini rugby at the club in the 1990s and has been club archivist for the last few years. He is also a member of the bowls section. In his writing, he has published widely on genealogy and the history of sport and traditional music. Keith lives in the Ashbrooke area of Sunderland in a street once inhabited by rugby players during the Victorian era.

Chapter One
Early Days - A Families' Affair (1873-1886)

Rugby football arrived in the town and port of Sunderland in County Durham at some point between 1864 and 1873. When a history of County Durham rugby was first written in the 1930s, the official date of the start of Sunderland RFC was noted as 1870 but at a later date this was revised to 1873. Evidence points to 1873 being the more likely starting point and, as a result, the club's centenary was celebrated in 1973 and its 125th anniversary in 1998.

The uncertainty about the club's origins is typical of much relating to the history of rugby football. What does seem clear is that by the time the club was formed, rugby had been played around the country in one form or another for the best part of half a century.

Rugby Football - the First Fifty Years

The start of rugby is fixed, rightly or wrongly, to the year 1823 and the poorly documented tale of how a young Rugby School pupil picked up a ball and ran with it. William Webb Ellis now has his name on the sport's World Cup - and that is a fact.

Despite the homage paid to Webb Ellis, many sports historians see various strands in the development of rugby in its early years. A number of variations of the game were played at public schools across England and were then taken on to the universities, especially to Cambridge. At the universities, interested players would gather and decide on a set of rules, with those used at Rugby School particularly popular. Against this background, a more traditional and less structured form of football was played from time to time in streets up and down the country. Many of these games were specific to Shrove Tuesday or 'Pancake Day'.

By the 1840s a recognisable set of laws was in place and by the 1860s, separate rugby clubs had sprung up in the London area. Guy's Hospital rugby dates back to 1843 while the earliest acknowledged club is Blackheath, formed in 1862. This club is still functioning today. In the 1860s too came meetings and heated discussions over the laws of the game, which led to some of the clubs preferring the kicking and dribbling game. Thus association football (or soccer, from the shortening of association) was born and the Football Association was set up - a number of years before rugby created its own national organisation.

The 1860s proved a busy time for both soccer and rugby. The oldest soccer league club in the world, Notts County, was established in the early 1860s while rugby clubs lay down roots in Lancashire, Yorkshire and the Midlands. However the game was still raw - played wherever an open space could be found - the laws were still uncertain, and changing rooms, showers and baths all luxuries of the future.

The years leading up to the formation of Sunderland RFC in 1873 witnessed an increase in rugby activity across the nation. In 1871, the English Rugby Union was set up - an indication that there was now enough interest to support a national organisation. Soon after, the first international between Scotland and England took place, the two major English universities began playing each other on a regular basis and the number of clubs applying for RFU membership increased; a sure sign that the sport was becoming increasingly popular.

Sunderland in 1873

When rugby came to Sunderland in the early 1870s, the then town and port was growing rapidly (Sunderland was granted city status in the late twentieth century). Its population was almost 100,000 at the time of the 1871 Census and the main jobs were in the coal mining and shipbuilding industries, and the maritime trade, with glass-making also an important occupation. The town had developed around the mouth of the River Wear and, by this time, was based on three separate parishes:

1. The old parish of Sunderland with its High Street. This lay just to the south of the river.
2. Monkwearmouth, so named because it had once housed a monastery, lay just to the north of the river.
3. Bishopwearmouth (the current city centre) lay to the south of the river and to the west of Sunderland parish.

The Newcastle Road headed off to the north, the Stockton Road to the south and the Chester Road (towards Chester-le-Street on the Great North Road) led off to the west, and the North Sea was to the east. The river had only been bridged locally in the late eighteenth century and, in 1873, had no railway crossing.

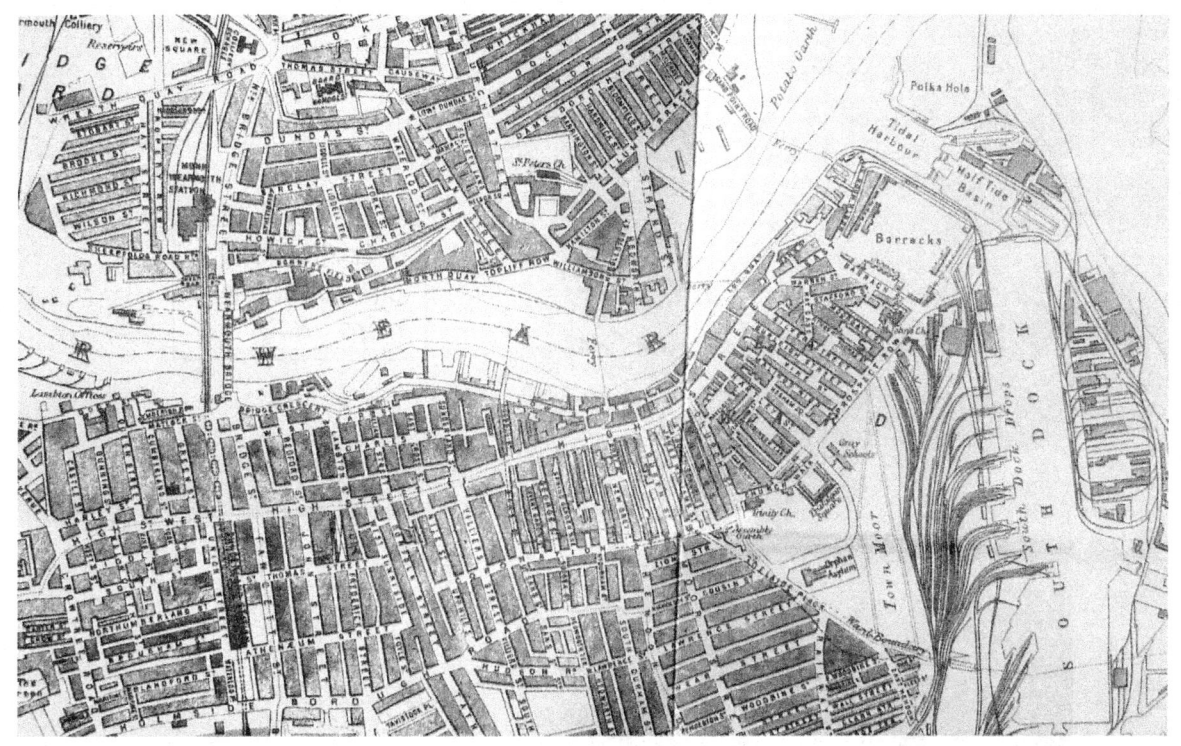

1.1: Sunderland in 1883 (with both railway and road bridge). The River Wear and North Sea (to the right) can be clearly seen

On the sporting front, cricket had already taken a grip in the town. There are newspaper accounts of games on Sunderland's Town Moor during the first years of the nineteenth century and Sunderland Cricket Club is now acknowledged to have been the first documented sports club formed in the Tyne and Wear area. It has been dated to 1834 under its initial name of Bishopwearmouth Cricket Club. Football, in its association form, had not taken such a grip and, as sports historian Mike Huggins has noted, Wearside was slower in this respect than its neighbours on the Tees and Tyne. It is therefore likely that there was not much in the way of organised team sport outside the summer months, although this was not so unusual at the time.

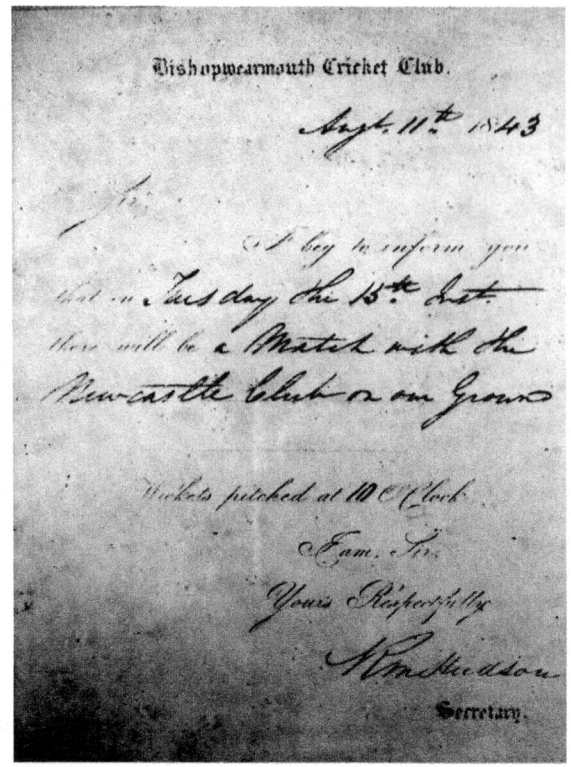

1.2: A cricket
club document
from 1843

Early Rugby in County Durham

By 1873, rugby football had already found its way into Sunderland's parent county, Durham. Commonly known as County Durham in order to differentiate it from the City of Durham, the county was much larger in the 1870s than it is today. Its major urban centres of Sunderland, South Shields, Gateshead, Darlington, Stockton and Hartlepool (then West Hartlepool and Old Hartlepool) now lie beyond its administrative bounds, though still within its limits as a sporting county.

As with the sport of rugby itself, the origins of Durham County rugby are somewhat misty. A version of the game seems to have been played at Durham School as early as 1851 and rugby was certainly established there by the 1860s. A rugby club was also set up in Darlington in the early part of that decade although it later embraced the association code before returning to the fold.

Games between the Darlington club and a selection of schoolboys and students from Durham were played and reported upon in the mid-1860s and these accounts give us a fascinating insight into the nature of the game around that time. It was played with 20 men on each side and its main feature was the scrimmage, described by the local press as 'a mass of struggling human beings' with the ball carrier buried at the bottom 'of a dozen others'. There were numerous ways of carrying the ball forward but under the 'Rugby' rules, hacking and tripping were both outlawed. By the early 1870s, informal get-togethers between players from Durham and compatriots from Yorkshire were taking place with written evidence for such games in 1871 and 1873.

Sunderland RFC - The First Game

On 30 December 1873, the *Sunderland Herald* reported a recent game of rugby played at Holmeside, the home of Sunderland Cricket Club (the name by which the original Bishopwearmouth Cricket Club, of 1834, was then known). It had been organised in the name of a club 'less than a week old' and was an organisation that had already attracted ninety members. A large crowd of spectators turned up to see the match.

The general history of the later Ashbrooke sports club has this game down as being between a Sunderland side and a 'pick-up' side. Pick-ups were common in the early universities when interested parties turned up to play and sides were picked out (or up) on the spot. The *Herald* reported that the game was between two sides chosen by Mr C Kidson and Mr H P Kayll. It was a lively contest and was not decided until the very last minute when Kidson scored a try. This was converted into a winning and all-important goal by Mr J Laing Jr.

This game is taken, rightly, in light of the press observations on 'a new club', to be the beginning of Sunderland RFC. This club has continued to play unbroken - except for war - since that game and has a justifiable claim, first made in the 1960s, to be the oldest continuous rugby club in north-eastern England. It would be churlish however, in respect to the vagaries of early records, not to recognise similar claims made by Durham City, Durham University and Houghton.

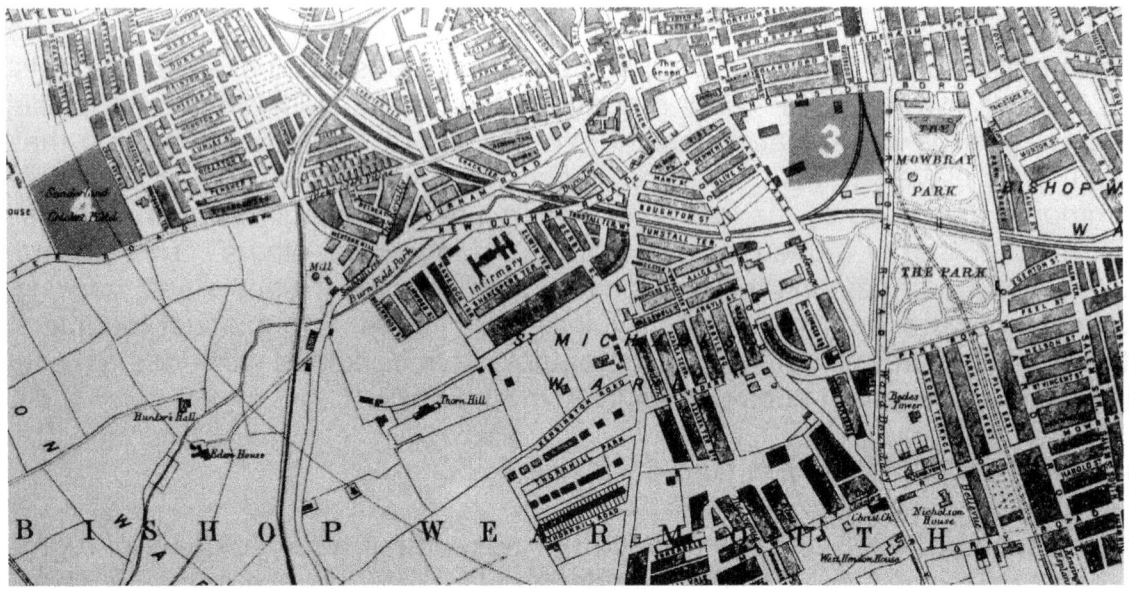

1.3: *Number 3 marks Holmeside – the cricket club's third ground and the rugby club's first. Number 4 marks the later ground at Chester Road Holmside Road also features on 1.1*

Although this was the club's first game, it was unlikely to have been the first game played in the town. Billy Kidson, rugby-playing brother of the Kidson mentioned in the *Herald* article, told club historians in the inter-war years that the game came to Sunderland soon after the cricket club started at Holmeside. This would be in the middle to late 1860s. He also credited its initial introduction to a 'player named James'. This may have been C H S James who turns up in both a playing and organisational capacity during the early days of Durham rugby. As a pupil at Durham School in the 1860s, he helped to organise the games with Darlington and was praised in the press for the quality of his play. There is no evidence as yet that he was in on the birth of the Sunderland club in 1873.

'A Families' Affair'

The press coverage of the first club game provides us with three names and these are most useful in giving us a real insight into the origins of the club. James Laing Jr. (b. April 1857), and his brother Arthur (b. February 1856) were involved in the club from the very start. Two of the sons of important Wearside shipbuilder James (later Sir James) Laing, they were both brought up within walking distance of the Holmeside ground. The 1871 Census of England and

Wales, however, reveals an even more fascinating fact about these two lads (for lads they were - even in 1873). In 1871, both were pupils at Wellington College in Berkshire. Here was a school that had adopted the rugby code with relish. In 1867, it had invited Oxford University to visit and play. In 1871, it had been a founder member of the RFU and had a representative on the organisation's first committee.

1.4: James Laing in 1882

1.5: Arthur Laing in 1882

Better still, the school's magazines for the early 1870s, *The Wellingtonian*, reveals that the Laing boys from Sunderland formed the lynch pin of the school side. Indeed James, the younger of the two, was captain of the side at one point. What better to do in the Christmas holiday, at home, than introduce friends to this relatively new game? Both of the Laing brothers missed out on the early seasons but they were in the side thereafter, as they returned home to work with their father in the shipbuilding industry. The earliest photograph of the club team, taken in 1874, only has 13 players. The two Laings were noted as absent. According to Wellington College records, they were back at school!

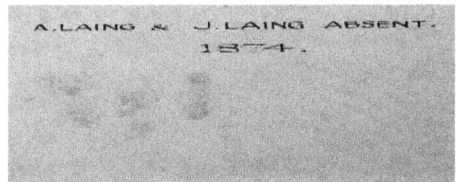

1.6: The absent Laings - pictorial evidence!

Then again it could have been the older men Kidson and Kayll who took the early initiative. Charles Kidson (b. c.1846) was a solicitor and the son of an attorney. He was in his mid-twenties when the club was formed and had been a boarder at Bramham College in Yorkshire as a teenager. Bramham College was a leading public school in the 1850s and 1860s but was closed down as result of a cholera outbreak. Evidence points to football being played at the school and to ex-pupils forming Bradford Rugby Club in 1863 (there is some dispute over whether it was the rugby game or the association game played at Bramham; in fact association seems the more likely). Kidson's attendance at the school may explain the strong links between Sunderland and Bradford and, indeed, Durham County and Yorkshire, which were to be forged later.

Hartley Perks Kayll (b. 1846) was the same age as Kidson. His father was a well known and successful Manx-born glass manufacturer and had served as Mayor of Sunderland. Hartley was born in London but others in the family were Wearside-born. He went to King William's College in the Isle of Man where he played rugby and may have played the game elsewhere in the 1862/3 season. By 1881, he had moved to London, making his career with the Sunderland club a relatively short one.

Another three 'founding fathers' were picked out by the authors of an earlier history of sport in Sunderland, "*To Ashbrooke and Beyond*" (hereinafter *TAAB*) – William Elliot (b. 1854), Francis Trewhitt (b. 1856) and Patrick Junor (b. 1852). Elliot was from a family of wealthy timber merchants who moved into the town centre from the outskirts. He attended Repton College, which stuck to the association code. He and his brother Charles turned to rugby and, in both cases, their skill with their feet was noted. There is a good chance that he was an early apostle of the sport in the town, as he played for the Durham County team before the club was formed. Francis Trewhitt was the same age as the Laing boys and a solicitor in training. There were family connections with Marlborough College here.

1.7: Thirteen of the first Sunderland XV 1874 - Charles Kidson with the ball

Junor had a real rugby pedigree. He moved to the Sunderland area just before the formation of the club to take up a position in a local brewery. He had been instrumental in the formation of Glasgow Academicals and was selected to play for Scotland against England in 1873 but had to miss the game due to business. Once he moved south, as the County's history points out, he virtually forfeited the right to play for his native country. Junor was later a driving force behind rugby in Houghton and the mining village of Tudhoe, and helped to forward the cause of back play in County Durham. His name crops up with the early games played by the Sunderland club although his actual role is not very clear.

The Kaylls, the Kidsons, the Laings and the Elliots provided the young club with a significant number of players thus justifying the 'families' affair' sub-title of this chapter. They were nearly all from the upper end of local society and had been sent off to public school. Many played rugby at school; some played the association game and simply moved across - possibly persuaded by friends. They also lived in the most prosperous area of the town - Ashbrooke. This was the first upper-middle class suburb to develop and lay just to the south of the Bishopwearmouth area and on both sides of the road leading out to the mining village of Ryhope and thence on to Stockton. The Kaylls, however, lived north of the river in affluent Roker Terrace close to the sea.

With these four families capable of providing up to two-thirds of a side at times, they are truly representative of early Sunderland RFC membership. Enjoying such social status, the club had generally more in common with clubs from the south of England than with those of Lancashire, Yorkshire and the Scottish borders where increasing numbers of players from the lower-middle and working classes were taking up the game.

The First Seven Seasons (1873-1880)

The year 1873 saw a number of new clubs starting up and joining the RFU, making Sunderland's formation part of a more general process (both Millom and Carlisle in the former county of Cumberland date back to the same year). Here was a game, although fifty years on, which was still suffering birth pangs and it was not unusual for players to turn out for more than one club when regular fixtures were not forthcoming. Many a club did not have a pitch or field of its own to play on and flitted from venue to venue. Nevertheless, clubs were springing up in Newcastle, South Shields and the Hartlepools and these were to provide stern opposition for the young Sunderland club.

The press account of Sunderland's first match suggested that a similar game was to be played on New Year's Day, 1874, but an account of that game has yet to turn up. Games against sides from Houghton, Darlington, Newcastle College of Physical Science and Northumberland were among the first played (Northumberland was a club or pick-up side; the county side did not emerge until 1880). The Northumberland match was reported in the *Sunderland Times*. It was played in December 1874 in very wintry conditions with Sunderland emerging as winners by one goal to nil. Both sides started off with only 14 men.

After three seasons at Holmeside, the cricket club was forced to move to a new ground. The current one was needed by the North Eastern Railway as part of the development of the new railway station, which opened a few years later. At the time, the town seemed to be advancing westward so the cricket club selected a ground on the Chester Road. It stood next to what was then the workhouse and is today the Sunderland Royal Infirmary. Chester Road remained the home of both the winter and summer sport until 1887.

During the first few seasons at Chester Road, the fixture list continued to grow although there were still only a handful of games per season. The theme of family and club can still be clearly seen in these years. Henry Kayll, younger brother of Hartley, was emerging as the club's first superstar and was joined on a regular basis by his brother John James. Alfred Kayll was also a regular and when the team was stuck for numbers on one memorable occasion, Andrew and Swinbourne Kayll made up the numbers. Six brothers played in the same side - remarkable yet, if truth be told, not a national or world record.

Charles Kidson's younger brother William Alexander (b. 1852) was known to all as Billy and was a regular from the start and, by all accounts, both a fine rugby player and a real character. He lived into the Second World War and provided historians of the time with much information about the formation of the club. Tales were told about him also, two of which featured separately in *TAAB*. On the first occasion after a good meal and a drink, he wandered across to Holmeside to watch a game and found one side had turned up short. He joined in as a half back with his trousers tucked into his shoes and his dress shirt on. The other tale appears almost too incredible to be true. Before another match, he borrowed a camel from a visiting circus and set up a plan to show up a cocky player from a visiting side (who was apparently disliked by his own colleagues). At the start of the game Kidson announced that there would be a special prize at the end of the game for the person who scored most tries. Both sides then made sure that the unpopular visitor was well supplied with the ball. He scored four tries and, at the end of the game, was presented with the camel on the pitch. What happened next was not recorded.

Anybody involved in rugby at club level will acknowledge that behaviour such as this has always been part and parcel of rugby football and to ignore it would be to deny a crucial aspect of the game - a comradeship at club level but one which often transcends inter-club rivalry.

There were also other sets of brothers - the Milbank Hudsons, the Reeds and the Manns. Ralph Milbank Hudson (b. c.1850) and Alfred (b. c.1856); Alfred was at public school in Darlington in 1871. The Reed brothers - Frederick, Rowland and Arthur - played together at one point. A C Mann and R J Mann appeared in the early 1870s.

Five other names cropping up on a regular basis were John Fowles (b. 1852), William Ogden (b. 1855), Bob Boyd, Henry Peters (b. 1854) and Edwin Scott (b. 1856). Fowles was a marine engineer and his father an engine designer, Ogden was in banking, Boyd an estate agent, Peters from a ship-owning family, as was Scott who was also a quarry manager. Nearly all lived in the large Victorian terraces in Ashbrooke. What is more, they were remarkably young. When playing their first matches for the club the Laings were 16 and 17, Scott 17, Peters and Ogden 18, as was one of the younger Kaylls. Evidence elsewhere also points to rugby clubs being set up by what were effectively enthusiastic teenagers who had played some form of organised ball team sport while at public school. There is also a possibility that Abel Chapman, later to become a world famous explorer, appeared for the club in its early days although this has yet to be verified.

1.8: An Ashbrooke Terrace

The Next Six Seasons (1880-1886)

The 1880/1 season has been selected as a cut-off point for good reason. It was the season in which the Durham County Challenge Cup was introduced. The idea of such a competition was appealing to young rugby clubs although the RFU preferred games to take place on a friendly basis (in the early 1880s, the RFU fought off a proposal for a national competition for clubs). Yorkshire had already set up its county competition and it had proved a real money-spinner, attracting large crowds. The Durham competition was based on the Yorkshire one. In addition, as sports historian Mike Huggins has pointed out, knockout competitions were a great focus for growing local pride as the soccer's FA Cup was beginning to prove.

During its lengthy existence, Sunderland RFC has only won the senior County Cup on a handful of occasions. In light of this, it could be argued that the club's main claim to fame is that it was victorious in the very first competition and a hand-tinted photograph of this cup-winning side has been the pride and joy of the club for well over a century. At the same time, it is wise not to get too carried away with this success. In the first round, opponents Durham University scratched. Fittingly, perhaps, it was Arthur Laing who recorded the very first try in the entire competition. The second round saw a victory over Darlington followed by a bye in the semi final. The final was played against local rivals Houghton.

According to the local *Chronicle*, Sunderland was declared the winner with three tries, one touch back and a dead ball to Houghton's touch back. In the article, covering the match, eight of the Sunderland players are mentioned by name. Arthur Laing, Billy Kidson and Henry Kayll missed conversions. Alfred M Hudson scored two of the tries while Oswald Thompson (b. 1861) and George Eden (b. 1853) combined for the third counter. Thompson was a member of a wealthy family of timber merchants which lived next door to the Kidson family. His brother Hugh (b. 1860) was also in the side. Sunderland-born Eden was a Church of England chaplain at the time of the game and later became the Bishop of Dover and Wakefield. He had attended Reading School and Cambridge University. His father was the rector of Bishopwearmouth. James Laing and Charles Kidson were also mentioned although it is clear from the report that the star performer was Henry Kayll.

Also in the side were John Fowles, Wilfred Gales (b. 1860) - a trainee solicitor - and William Dickinson (b. 1856) - son of a marine engine builder. Douglas Inman (b. 1863) was a trainee engineer visiting the Thompson family, and Robert Hitchcock (b. 1860) was the son of the vicar of Whitburn and later to join the church himself. Clearly rugby football had church approval; at one point at least three vicar's sons were in the Sunderland First XV.

1.9: Sunderland's cup winning side

-21-

This was a good period for the fixture list, with fixtures home and away to strong Yorkshire sides Halifax and Bradford. Of five fixtures with these clubs, three were won, one drawn and only one lost. Other opposition included Edinburgh Institution and Richmond. A few months after the cup victory, Charles Kidson died. He was 34 and his obituary noted the debt the club owed him.

Anatomy of a Season - 1882/3

Billy Kidson left the club his fixtures' book for this season, which enables us to have a good look at exactly what was going on at the time. During the season, the club fielded a 1st and 2nd XV and hosted a county trial match. The season ran from mid-October to March with the last few fixtures left open for the County Cup.

1.10: The cover of Billy Kidson's book

The 1st XV had ten home and eight away fixtures lined up for the 1882/3 season. Northern, Tynemouth and Northumberland from the county of Northumberland were played on a home and away basis, as were Durham clubs - City, Westoe, Darlington and Hartlepool. York, Bradford, Tynedale and Edinburgh Institution made up the other fixtures. The 2nd XV had eight home fixtures all with away returns. Five were against the 2nd XVs of Northern, Hartlepool, Westoe, Northumberland and Tynemouth with the other three against local junior sides Sunderland Rovers and Humbledon (both south of the river) and Boldon (to the north).

As it is interesting to note the ages of those playing, so it is to reflect on the ages. The club's organisers and committee members are listed on the cover of the fixture card. Arthur Laing (25) was chairman, Billy Kidson (30) captain and James Laing (26) vice captain. Francis Trewhitt (25) was secretary and the remainder of the committee was made up of Charles Elliot (19), Oswald Thompson (21), Gales (22), Dickinson (26) and the two Hudsons (32 and 26). Two of the three rugby playing Reed brothers (23 and 21) and Charles Lilburn (41) complete the picture. The secretary, Herbert Webster (20), was a cousin of the Laing boys and son of an iron merchant and county magistrate. Lilburn, an older man, was from a family of coal fitters (middlemen in the coal industry). He was also descended from John Lilburn the famous radical leveller of the seventeenth century Civil War. The average age was low – early to mid 20s and eleven out of the fourteen committee members were regular first team players.

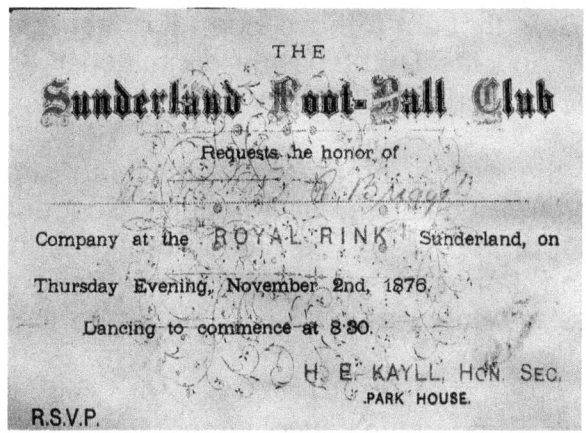

1.11: An early social event

The club's time at Chester Road also saw two experiments with floodlighting. Although this may come as something of a surprise to modern readers, there is evidence of other similar experiments around the same time - at Broughton Rugby Club in Manchester, for example. The Chester Road experiments were slightly amusing and carried out with the aid of someone connected to the lighthouse at nearby Souter Point. In 1880, four floodlights were set up for an 'electric light game' but heavy snow prevented the use of all of them. Later in the same year, the lights, operated by a traction engine, produced an effect, which ranged from 'brilliant' to the hardly visible – reminiscent in some way of the modern soccer coverage provided by some foreign satellite stations.

The County Arrives

Players from the Sunderland club had considerable roles to play in the development of county rugby. The Durham County Union was established in 1876 and became the first county union to join the RFU as a body in the 1882/3 season. Interestingly there are signs of an earlier county side prior to 1876 and of Sunderland involvement there too.

Yorkshire was the first county to get its house in order and it is now clear that games were played against scratch sides formed from Durham players in the early 1870s. These games have the feel of Easter tour matches about them and were probably set up through an old boy network of former public school boys. A 20-a-side match took place between Durham and Yorkshire at Darlington in 1871 and another match is recorded just prior to the formation of the Sunderland club. The latter match, played in 1873, is thought to have been the first county 15-a-side game played in the country and the Durham side contained William Elliot, soon to be a founder member of Sunderland RFC.

Between 1873 and the formation of the county proper, at least three similar games took place between Durham and Yorkshire, all featuring Sunderland players. The Durham side won two out of the three. The Kidson brothers, three of the Kaylls (Hartley, Henry and John James) made appearances along with William Elliot. Billy Kidson scored tries in two of the games. Peters and Ogden also featured.

Between 1876 and the first County Cup, Sunderland's involvement in the county setup remained strong. There were still few sides to choose from and Sunderland was a senior club. As an official County Championship got underway, matches with Yorkshire and Lancashire took place with the larger counties victorious. There were usually between five and nine Sunderland players in the county side including the Kidsons, Kaylls and Laings with Henry Kayll increasing his reputation game by game. Popular estate agent Bob Boyd, John Fowles and Alfred Hudson also played, alongside one or two others.

The Chester Road ground hosted matches against a pre-Northumberland XV and Yorkshire. The Yorkshire game, fully reported in the local press, was the one in which nine Sunderland players featured; it also showed the strength of the larger Yorkshire county. The game proved a 'remarkably easy victory for the visitors'. It was played in four twenty-minute segments with the wind from the Pavilion End a major factor. Kirkstall, Bradford, Hull, Huddersfield and Leeds had representatives in their county's side. Named players included internationals such as Harry Huth of Huddersfield, Harry Garnett of Bradford and G Harrison of Hull. After the game there was a grand dinner and a sing-song. Charles Kidson made a speech about the good relations between Sunderland and the Yorkshire clubs, underlining his Yorkshire public school background as a factor in the development of the club.

Sunderland continued to contribute players to the county side between 1880 and the club's move away from Chester Road in 1887, although numbers dwindled slightly as new clubs became established. The period also saw the beginning of matches against Northumberland County proper and Cumberland with the first official local derby between Durham and Northumberland played at the Chester Road ground.

The Laing brothers, Billy Kidson and Henry Kayll all crop up alongside new names from the club. Brothers Rowland and Frederick Reed were among them, as was a second member of the Elliot family, Charles, and the first member of the influential Cox family, Burdon - only 18 years of age when first selected for the county. At one point there was a match between the veterans of Durham and the veterans of Northumberland in which Billy Kidson, Alfred Hudson, William Dickinson and Wilfred Gales took part, alongside the mysterious Patrick Junor.

Just prior to leaving Chester Road, the club had the honour of hosting the first county match against the mighty Middlesex. There were six Sunderland players in the side including Charles Elliot and young Burdon Cox.

At this point it is worth reflecting on the importance of the county structure in rugby. Up until fairly recently it formed part of the build up to higher representative rugby in a way it never did in association football. A county cap was highly prized and was usually worn in team photographs.

Trialists and Internationals

From the county level there were two further steps up the ladder of rugby playing success and a number of early Sunderland players mounted that ladder. These higher rungs consisted of the trial and the international. Like hockey, rugby adopted a regional system in its early international trials - in this case North v South.

In 1878 Henry Kayll was selected to play for the North and it is clear why. From the very first season of the club, his name was the one which appeared most in press reports both at club and county level. His selection along with another Durham player made him one of the first Durham-born men to play representative rugby. A successful trial led to his selection for the England v Scotland match in the same year.

1.12: Henry Kayll - Sunderland strip and England cap

The match was scoreless and was the last home international between the two countries before the Calcutta Cup was introduced. It was also Kayll's only international appearance although contemporary rugby historian Frank Marshall described him not long after as one of the finest backs of his day. The England-Scotland match itself was a damp squib. Played at The Oval in March, it ended pointless. Kayll played at full back and accompanying him in the backs was the famous Lancashire and England cricketer A N Hornby.

Charles Elliot, whose career developed a little later than Henry Kayll's, also benefited from a good trial and was selected to play for England against Wales at Blackheath during the 1885/86 season. England ran out winners and the same Frank Marshall as mentioned above commented wryly on Elliot's contribution to the victory:

'In the Welsh match he specially distinguished himself by a foolish piece of play which luckily proved to be the winning point of the match. Following hard up, he caught the ball from a bad screw kick of the Welsh full back and made his mark instead of going for the try. That style of play may win applause in Durham but it met with emphatic and forcible expression of disapproval from the England captain and the 'finished' players of the south. Stoddart took the place kick and scored a goal so the laugh at the finish was on Elliot's side.'

v. Yorkshire, at Leeds, November 19th, 1887.

1.13: Charles Elliot (middle centre with moustache) in charge of Durham County

With this description we are allowed a fascinating insight into the way the game was played and clearly making a mark and taking a pot at goal was an accepted way of scoring - if not regarded as the 'manly' thing to do (one is reminded here of the way modern crowds treat the taking of the occasional penalty kick when the ball could have been run). This proved to be Elliot's only international appearance. Ironically, if Stoddart is labelled as one of the 'finished' players of the south, this famous cricket and rugby player was born in South Shields!

Playing the Game

Interesting as the early history of Sunderland RFC may be, there is some need for caution. A number of the early photographs of the players are so modern and realistic that it is possible to be lulled into a false sense of security when it comes to imagining them playing the game. In fact, the game they played must have been very different from the one we watch and play today.

As hinted at earlier in this chapter, for the majority of these early seasons, rugby was dominated by trundling forward play. This was true of both the 20-a-side and 15-a-side versions of the game. Most of the sketches drawn in the days before photography show a 'struggling mass of humanity' trying to capture and progress the ball both at school and club level. Also whereas the modern player is encouraged to 'get low' in fixed and loose forward play, this was looked down upon in mid-Victorian times and gentlemen stood tall and straight and simply pushed hard when involved in the scrimmage. When the ball emerged from this mass, the job of the back was to pick it up and head for the line. When his progress was impeded (usually by an opposition back tackling) then it was straight back to the scrimmage.

It is also clear that there was no concept of linking play between forwards and backs or even between backs and backs. Thus the pass was very much a thing of the future. The standard set up behind the forwards was two players 'half-back', a single player 'three-quarters-back' and two players 'full-back'. In a sense this was more like the standard American form of football with its running backs.

Though fun to play in for those who enjoyed a good tussle or a good run, the game must have been fairly boring for spectators and the moves away from this style of play are dateable and understandable. In 1878, a law was passed ordering the ball to be released on tackle. This ensured that it became less tied up in hand during the scrimmage. Harry Vassall, Oxford University trainer, is seen as the first man to encourage the playing of the ball through hands. Some books point to the year 1881 and the North-South trial as the very first occasion upon which a pass was made between a half-back and the three-quarter. By the middle of the 1880s, this movement had led to the use of four three-quarters -

two on the wing and two in the centre - and thus to a formation we recognise today.

Equally the method of gaining victory in a rugby match has changed. At times during the early days of Sunderland RFC even the players must have been confused as to how to go about winning a match. Initially the only counter was the goal – scored by kicking the ball between the posts after a try had been put down. Plenty of tries but no goals meant a draw. This was changed so that both tries and touch backs behind your own line counted in the event of no goal being scored. Even so, the goal remained king over everything else.

It was 1886 before the idea of awarding points or 'the Cheltenham system' was adopted, i.e., the very last season in which Sunderland RFC used the Chester Road ground. The try was awarded a point and a conversion three points (points that absorbed the single point for the try). The scoring at matches played under this system tended to be low compared to the scores of today. Throughout the 1870s, an umpire from each side marshalled the games. Neutral umpires were introduced in 1881 and referees in 1885.

These explanations should help us to understand more clearly how Sunderland came out victors in the very first County Cup final in 1881. The team managed to cross the opposition line on four occasions but the tries scored were not converted into goals. Three separate kickers missed attempts and the fourth try was put down as a 'dead ball' as it was decided that the throw in to the preceding lineout had been crooked. Being forced to touch down behind one's own line also counted against a side at the time. This happened to both sides in the final once while Arthur Laing 'obviated the necessity' of another counter against Sunderland by kicking clear. Today the result of such touchbacks would be an offensive five-metre scrum.

Fortunately, by 1881, the days had passed when converted goals alone counted and thus Sunderland was declared the winner with three tries, one touch back and a dead ball to Houghton's touch back. In the very early days, the lack of goals would have resulted in a drawn game.

SRFC and SAFC

It would be criminal to ignore the opportunity of examining the developing relationship between rugby and what we now know as football, as it was a relationship key to an understanding of the history of both games. Anyone who travels today will recognise the high esteem in which English league football is held and relative success in that league system has made Sunderland Association Football Club (SAFC) a household name all over the sporting world. Capable of defeating the best sides in the country (on a good day) and regularly packing in between 40,000 and 50,000 supporters at its state-of-the-art Stadium of Light, SAFC exists in a very different world from SRFC. It was not ever thus!

When organised rugby came to Sunderland in 1873, there was little, if any, sign of the association game. Mike Huggins, vastly knowledgeable on north-eastern sport, often points to the arrested development of the association game on Wearside. It always trailed behind the Tyne area (which eventually gave birth to Newcastle United) and the Tees area (which provided Middlesbrough with a home).

Sunderland AFC traces its roots back to 1879 and to the Hendon area of the town. Here a young Scottish teacher called James Allan returned from holiday in Scotland full of enthusiasm for the round-ball game. With fellow teachers and some pupils, he set up the side, which is SAFC today. Hendon lies on the same side of the river as the Chester Road cricket and rugby ground, and slightly east of the Ashbrooke area where most of the rugby players lived. In some cases, the footballers lived in streets adjacent to the rugby players yet there was a clear gulf in class. With one or two exceptions, the footballers lived in the lower-middle class terraces - in homes managed by a single servant who did not 'live in'. Beside teachers, they were clerks and shopkeepers and the children of the same.

Like many an early rugby club, the football team had trouble finding a permanent home ground. After two or three attempts to settle, they arranged a home at The Grove, Ashbrooke, on land owned by the proprietor of the Sunderland Echo. This was in the 1882 season. Today that field is part of the Ashbrooke ground, home of the rugby club for well over a century, and a blue plaque is displayed at the club entrance acknowledging the football-rugby link.

The football club lasted only one season at The Grove before heading north of the river where it has remained ever since. The 'blue plaque project' led to research into the reasons for the move and the accepted outcome is that football was driven out by rugby. The Ashbrooke area was essentially upper-middle class and devoted to the oval ball game. At one point there were at least three rugby sides playing within a short distance of each other: Sunderland,

Sunderland Rovers and Humbledon. The football club's move towards the shipyards and mines north of the river was, within time, to prove its making.

Although differences rather than similarities have been stressed here, it would be foolish not to note one notable similarity. Both clubs were the brainchildren of enthusiastic youngsters. James Allan and his team contained many teenagers and Allan himself was only 19 at the formation of the club. Rugby's influential Laing brothers, it is worth recalling, went back to school after playing in the club's initial game.

And one final musing note on the football front. With a little more luck, Sunderland Rugby Football Club may have enrolled the help of one of the great men of association football. Charles Alcock fits the bill in almost every respect when it comes to early Sunderland rugby players. His birthplace in Norfolk Street, Sunderland, lies close to a house in which a later rugby club's committee met. He would have just turned 30 when the club was formed. In 1851, he was living in fashionable town centre John Street, where the rugby club was to hold other committee meetings. He was destined to go to public school and may have returned full of enthusiasm for the game of rugby, as did many of his Sunderland contemporaries. He didn't; neither did his Sunderland-born parents. The family moved to Chingford in Essex. Charles played the association game and went to Harrow School. The rest of the story is told in books and on websites. Charles Alcock became 'Mr Football' and was the leading force behind the FA Cup, international football, league football and professionalism in the game. He also made a massive contribution to the development of organised first-class cricket.

If only!

Some Conclusions

The title of this book, 'One Among Many', was chosen to reflect over a century of Sunderland RFC's history. With some pride, it is possible to conclude that the club was a little more than one among many in its early days. By the end of the 1886/7 season, Sunderland RFC was a major force in north-eastern sport, boasting international players and hosting important county matches. It was in charge of organised winter team sports south of the river, and had driven the association game out. In most of the games covered by the local press Sunderland Football Club meant the rugby club and the words 'Sunderland Football Club' were embossed on rugby club material for many years to come.

Reports on the round ball game had to use the term Sunderland Football Club (Association) and the space afforded to their efforts in the newspapers was much smaller in comparison to rugby.

By the end of the 1886/7 season, most of the players playing rugby for Sunderland RFC were still from the prosperous end of society - top businessmen, former public schoolboys and sons of the church. Many of them lived in the leafy upper-middle class Ashbrooke suburb, which goes a long way toward explaining that which happened next.

Chapter Two
Doubts, Decisions and a Dash of Glory (1887-1914)

On 30 May 1887 a big athletic festival was held to celebrate the opening of the new Ashbrooke sports ground. The ground had been constructed as home to what was now called The Sunderland Cricket and Football Club. By the end of the century, the wider club had also set up sections for hockey, tennis and bowls. These sections were known in their individual sporting worlds as Sunderland Hockey Club, Sunderland Lawn Tennis Club and Sunderland Bowls Club. Well over a century later, Ashbrooke Sports Club (as the wider club is now known) remains the parent body for all these clubs - a remarkable Victorian survival. For the club's rugby section, still operating as Sunderland Rugby Football Club, the first twenty-five years at the new ground were among the most interesting in the club's history.

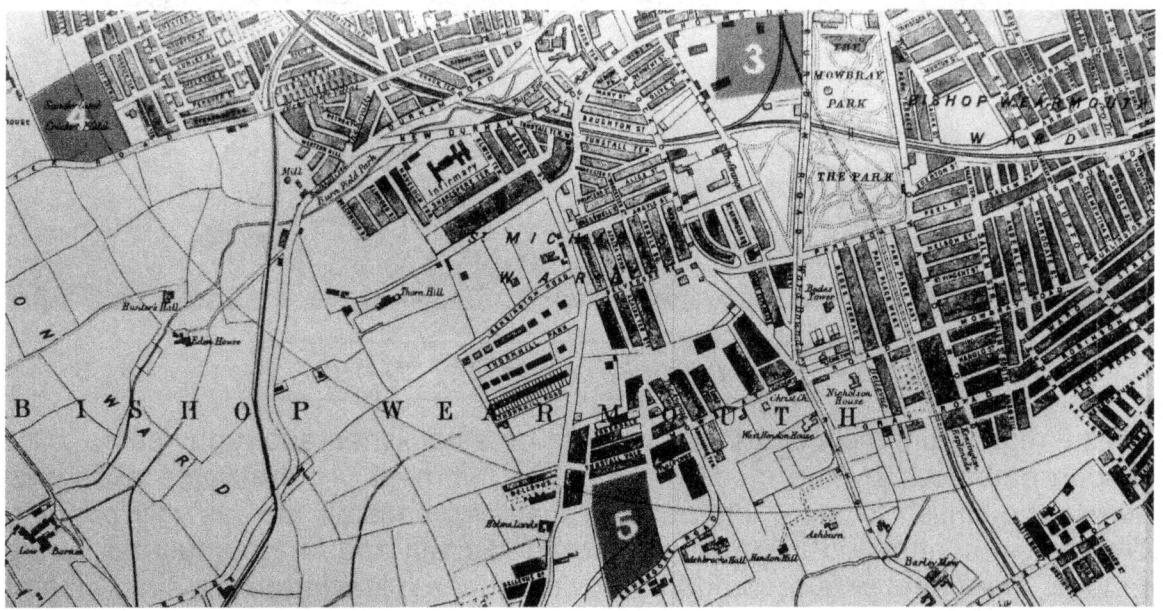

2.1: Ashbrooke
(No. 5)

The move to Ashbrooke came at a time when organised sport was extremely popular. The developing towns and cities were bustling. Muscular Christianity and public health concerns combined to encourage men and, increasingly, women to take up sport. In addition to the sports mentioned above, cycling, golf and swimming had great support leading to a Golden Age in many British sports during the Edwardian period (1901-1910).

2.2: Ashbrooke opens May 30, 1887

On the rugby front, new clubs continued to be established and rugby came to be a sport embraced by the modern Olympic movement. As the game expanded across the British Empire, international matches became increasingly popular. Touring sides attracted large crowds both in Britain and in the countries of the Empire. The game was recorded in moving images, leaving us an even clearer picture of how it was played (forwards, for example, still seemed to lurch slowly from set piece to set piece). Within a decade of the move to Ashbrooke, the 'modern' setup of forwards and backs was firmly in place as was a new points system that awarded three points for a try, two for a conversion, three for a penalty goal and four for a drop goal (although for a short time, international rugby adopted a slightly different scoring system).

Not all was sweetness and light. Within a decade of the move to Ashbrooke, a major dispute arose in the rugby world over the future of the game. For some clubs, especially those in the north-west of England, amateur friendlies and cup matches held little interest. Large crowds for cup matches showed that the game was capable of arousing great interest and of making enough money to reward working class players for the 'broken time', when they were missing paid work in order to attend games and training. A league system would strengthen the game further and give the followers of successful sides another way of boasting that 'local pride', considered so important by sports historian Mike Huggins. The organisers of the national game at the RFU disagreed with the idea of paying players and voted out the idea of leagues and professionalism on more than one occasion.

Payment of one sort or another (often called 'boot money') had gone on for some time in clubs favouring the new approach. They were suspended and banned from time to time. During the early to mid 1890s it all came to a head. In 1895, over twenty clubs broke away from the RFU and set up a separate Northern Rugby Union. By the following year, the new union had a membership of 59. At first the game they played was the same as the old one but with time what we now know as Rugby League developed. In the 1890s it was simply about leagues and the payment of players for training and playing time.

For those who remained with the union game, there were changes too. The RFU drew up battle lines and a strict code of conduct in relation to the amateur game; it also developed a less organised anti-league policy.

While this was happening (or, in fact, slightly before it), the association game had already grasped the nettle of leagues and professionalism. Under the guidance of Sunderland-born public schoolboy Alcock (see Chapter One) the Football Association had given the payment of players its blessing and the Football League had begun to operate.

For Sunderland RFC, as for many similar clubs, this was a time for doubts and decisions. Should it follow other northern clubs into a league system? Should it abandon the oval ball completely and move to the round ball and association? In the latter case, the rugby club's association rival north of the river had shown the way forward. Sunderland AFC had grown steadily in the 1880s and had thrust itself into the new league system. While the rugby row was heating up, Sunderland AFC and Aston Villa became the Manchester United and Chelsea of their day. From relative obscurity, Sunderland AFC moved up to take league titles in 1892, 1893 and 1895. The poor relatives had now become the successful ones, packing in the crowds at their latest ground on Newcastle Road. When a history of sport was published in 1895, Sunderland AFC was held up as the glowing example of successful professional association football. What was the rugby club going to do about it?

Casting Doubts and Making Decisions

It is clear from the start that professionalism had little support at Sunderland RFC in the early 1890s. All the pointers from 1873 onwards are towards upper-middle class involvement in the sport in the town and a lack of need for 'broken time' payments. Among the papers in the Ashbrooke archive is a set relating to the new regulations regarding amateurism issued by the RFU in the autumn of 1895. This includes a draft copy for consideration and has the odd handwritten note on it. 'Agreed to' was the most common handwritten entry and the only dispute appears to have been over the role of the referee in sniffing out professionalism. From some of the suggestions agreed to it would seem to have been an unforgiving set of regulations as witnessed by the following extracts from the original printed sheet:

1. Professionalism is illegal;

2. Acts of professionalism are:

   1) By an individual –

      A. Asking, receiving or relying on a promise to receive any money consideration whatever actual or prospective; any employment or advancement; any establishment in business; or any compensation whatever for –

         (a) Playing football, or rendering any service to a football organisation;
         (b) Training or loss of time therewith;
         (c) Compensation for time lost in playing football or in travelling in connection with football;
         (d) Expenses in excess of the amount actually disbursed on account of reasonable hotel or travelling expenses.

If individuals playing the game in Sunderland did not need the money, the club certainly did and this is where the problem lay. Funds had to be raised in order to play rugby at all and the parent sports club itself was in financial trouble in the mid 1890s (see Appendix One). The paying crowds had gone to watch association football. Looking back at the previous decade, the rugby club secretary noted in the 1890s:

> "As the association game had not then developed into the popular favourite which is one of the wonders of today, the rugby game received a far greater share of support from the public."

Under the system of rugby then in existence, the only real money-spinner was the County Cup. In 1896 a decision was taken to charge all club members at the gate for cup-ties (members of the general public were already charged). The entrance fee was to be 6d (six old pence), and it cost an extra 6d to transfer into the stand. At the same time a plea was put to the wider club's governing board (hereinafter simply 'governing board') to establish turnstiles in order to ensure payment. Turnstiles were put in - nine years later.

One of the major outlays of the club was on travelling expenses. The RFU acknowledged the need to pay 'reasonable' expenses for travel and accommodation (and in the case of Sunderland RFC accommodation rarely, if ever, came into the equation - the vast majority of fixtures were local). This payment created difficulties at club level. In 1897, a motion was passed declaring that players could only claim after they had paid their memberships (this has been a very common problem throughout the history of the game!). Three years later, the governing board asked if players could possibly pay their own travel expenses. The terse written reply from the rugby committee was "no expenses, no team". In 1906, however, general club finances hit rock bottom and the players agreed to pay their own expenses. How long this lasted is not clear.

Another possibility was an amateur league within the county or within the joint counties of Northumberland and Durham. This would ratchet up local rivalry and possibly attract larger paying audiences. In 1896, a junior club, Westoe Wednesday, suggested a league structure. The Sunderland club committee rejected this. In the following year, Northumberland club Wallsend suggested a joint county league. A meeting was held and the Sunderland club sent representatives. At the ensuing county meeting they voted, successfully, for rejection. This was "on the ground that" it was "a step in the direction of professionalism". The club committee accepted a third league proposal in 1898 by six votes to one. This league, for Durham County alone, would exist for both 1st XVs and 2nd XVs. In the words of the club secretary, the move was 'quashed' by the RFU. Organisation of the league had clearly been at an advanced stage because the club was told by an RFU official to throw out its proposed fixtures and to "make the usual fixtures during the following season". Leagues frightened the RFU as they appeared to lead to professionalism, and rugby union, as it was now known, was strictly an amateur game.

The league idea at county level refused to go away; it was considered and rejected at club level in 1900. At the end of the 1902/3 season, however, the secretary noted triumphantly that the club had ended "second in the league table" and that "since last season the Durham and Northumberland Union have installed an inter-club Championship". This had "greatly increased the interest in the matches of the various clubs". He also wrote that club finances had improved and would have been even better had it not been for the bad weather. In an interesting final analysis he added three other favourable outcomes of the league games:

1. Matches started more punctually;
2. Matches were more keenly contested;
3. There was no difficulty in getting players to play on a regular basis.

He also indicated that the 1st XV had played 19 games in the inter-club league, had won 11 and drawn one, with 132 points for and 131 against.

A brief typewritten article in the Ashbrooke archives confirms the existence of this league. The article was put together when the Courage Leagues were being introduced in the late 1980s. "In some parts of the country, leagues are not a new venture", the writer notes, "One such area is Durham County and its neighbour Northumberland where League football was in operation from the first years of the century and at junior club level lasted until the depression years of the thirties".

By a pure quirk of fate, a pristine copy of the rules and regulations for this league has survived - used as a page marker in a club minute book many years later. The league is disguised as 'Durham and Northumberland Inter-County Club Championships' and the regulations for the 1904/5 season stated that at least eight "home and home" matches (presumably home and away) had to be played with two points for a win and one for a draw. Positions in the championship table were awarded on a percentage win basis. The clear aim of the league was to attract more spectators with the starting of matches on time a real priority.

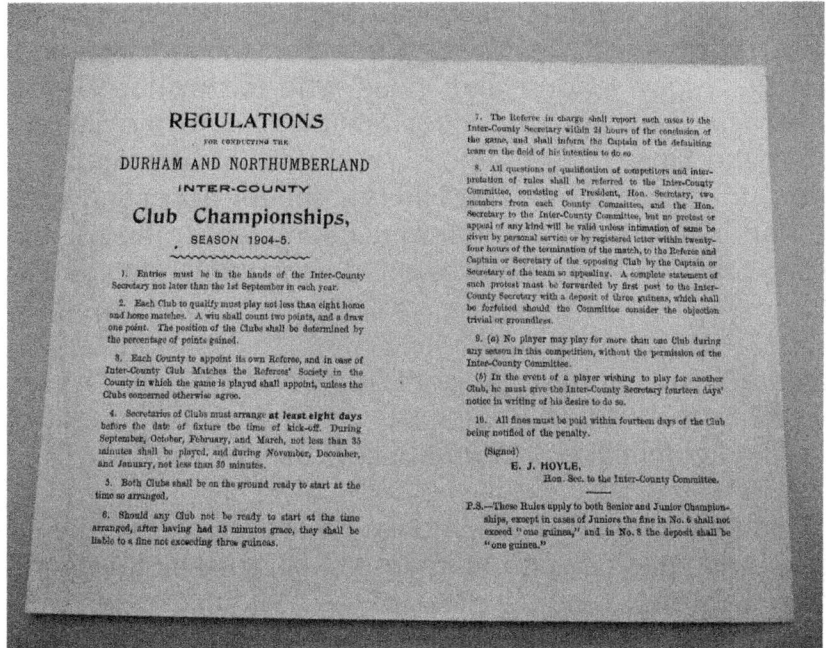

2.3: Regulations for the league

The club minutes for the 1903/4 season back up the existence of this twin counties' league. There are references to claiming points for cancelled matches and not playing league games on county days. In 1904, Northumbrian side Old Novos claimed two points because Sunderland had cancelled a game. In the same year Sunderland's 2nd XV was withdrawn from its league only to be returned in the 1905/6 season. In the 1906/7 season, there were occasional references in the minutes to the 1st XV being in some form of league system.

The wider spread of professionalism in rugby affected the committee of Sunderland RFC on two further occasions, both involving what might be considered interesting cases and both leading to direct communication with the RFU.

The Gould Case was a cause-celèbre in the days following the big split between union and league. The admirers of Arthur Gould, a popular Welsh rugby union international, presented him with a house. The RFU decreed that this was the equivalent of a 'monetary testimonial'. Although the Welsh Committee withdrew its £50 donation from the house fund, the RFU was still annoyed and banned its member clubs from playing any side for which Gould had been selected. They also refused to allow him to play for English clubs. The case went on for almost eighteen months at which point Gould decided to accept the testimonial. The rugby world was divided between those frightened by the professionalism of the rugby league and those who felt sympathy for Gould and the Welsh committee, as the laws over testimonials in the Welsh game were quite unclear at the time. In September 1897, the following private proposition was put forward for consideration by RFU members accepting that Gould's actions had been an 'act of professionalism', circumstances had been 'exceptional' and suggesting that he should be allowed to continue to play under the auspices of the RFU.

The minutes of the Sunderland RFC committee and the governing board show how complex and divisive this case was. In September 1897, the RFU proposal was read out to the Sunderland committee and written down as follows:

> "That Mr A J Gould having accepted a testimonial in the form that the Committee of the Rugby Union has decided to be an act of professionalism nevertheless under the exceptional circumstances of the case, the meeting recommends the Committee to allow him to play against clubs under their management."

The club committee was much divided over its response to this RFU memo. At the club meeting where there was "a small attendance", it was resolved to send a representative to the national meeting to support the proposal. A week later a motion was put forward to rescind the last one and to inform Rowland Hill, Secretary of the RFU, the *Athletics News* and the *Sunderland Post and Echo*. This motion was defeated on the casting vote of the chairman. The originator of the amendment then proposed a special meeting to discuss the case further. This was defeated by eight votes to three. That wasn't the end of the matter. The wider club's governing board stepped in and said that the rugby club's original declaration of support for reinstating Gould was 'null and void' and that this too should be reported in the *Athletics News, Yorkshire Post* and the local papers.

According to the national histories similar heated debates took place everywhere. In August 1900, after almost three years of controversy, the Welsh laws on rugby professionalism were brought into line with the English ones and, as the RFU centenary history puts it, "so closed the great Gould case". How Sunderland RFC voted in the end is unclear.

2.4: The Gould Case - Sunderland RFC
committee minutes

The Meek Case was a local issue but one which may have been repeated at club level elsewhere. In September 1901, the secretary of Sunderland RFC wrote to the RFU requesting the reinstatement to the Rugby Union of a Mr A R

Meek. He had recently moved into the area, wanted to play for Sunderland and had previously played for Goole in the Northern Union. A general letter from the RFU came in reply stating that a motion of the same month had been passed "classing as professionals all players who signed a Northern Union form". With it was a copy of an individual letter sent to Mr Meek and signed by Rowland Hill to the effect that there could be "no exception to the rule against reinstatement". Meek's name has not yet been found in any of the Sunderland sides of the period.

A trawl through the minutes for this period reveals little if any sign of 'shamamateurism' or veiled professionalism at Sunderland RFC. In truth, the club could not afford it. Clearly it had not followed the ways of some of its former allies in Yorkshire and Lancashire, and fixtures with old rivals like Halifax had been lost to the rugby league system. At the same time, the constant debate over the upgrading of cup games and the drive towards an amateur league structure separates the club from its upper-middle class compatriots in the south who preferred the friendlies. Despite a stated opposition to professionalism, however, some of these compatriots have since been shown to have been generous with 'personal expenses'.

Of equal interest to the topic of professionalism is the revelation that a move by the club to play association football was not out of the question. Other rugby clubs (notably Darlington and Bradford) changed codes and the national success of Sunderland AFC bore down heavily on the local rugby club. This is made perfectly clear in an end of season report for 1904:

> "We regret that the gate receipts are not so large as they might have been possibly due to the bad weather and the fact that Sunderland Association Club matches fell in many cases on the same day as our best fixtures."

History teaches that large urban towns and cities could accommodate more than one association side (take Nottingham, Bristol and Liverpool for example) and the signs were that if a professional game were to be adopted at all then 'soccer' was the one to go for. In 1890 a proposal was put to the club AGM to move to the association game "with a view to increasing the income". A group of 1st XV players led the successful opposition. In 1905 a sterner challenge was issued. Vehemently supported by an influential rugby/hockey player and a well-respected county rugby player, the motion was that the club should "play under the rules and directions laid down by the Football Association".

The arguments put forward by the pro-associationists make for convincing reading. They claimed that rugby had little support in the area and that public interest was dying off. At the same time, the public schools were said to be contemplating changing codes as parents were complaining about the roughness of rugby football. Intriguingly, the same argument was being put forward at that time in the United States in connection with the outlawing of 'American Football'. The game continued thanks to law changes. Ironically the opposition in the USA had suggested that the colleges play rugby instead!

Meanwhile back at Ashbrooke, the pro-rugby group, led by those who had forced through the earlier rejection, argued that the general club owed its very existence to the game of rugby football. The pro-rugby group carried the day by 70 votes to 15. The discussions held at Sunderland RFC during the period were of enough interest to be mentioned by Tony Collins in his important work *A Social History of English Rugby Union*.

Three years later, a highly organised campaign to bring association football to the club nearly succeeded. On this occasion it was suggested that an amateur side should be entered in a local league - and not at the expense of rugby. This suggestion was taken seriously and led to a working party. In the end the move was rejected mainly because of lack of space (a perennial Ashbrooke problem). The ground had effectively a single rugby pitch (one third of the grassed area, while the other two thirds were permanently dedicated to cricket and hockey). The club was also operating three rugby sides by this time. Case dismissed.

So doubts had been expressed and decisions made. By 1910, it was clear that Sunderland RFC would continue to operate playing the amateur game of rugby football as the rugby section of the wider Ashbrooke setup. This remains the situation over a century later.

On the Field

The authors of the 1960s *To Ashbrooke and Beyond* divided the first twenty five years of rugby at the new ground into three sections – 1887 to 1896, 1897 to 1907 and 1907 until the outbreak of war in 1914. It is a division that works well.

1887 - 1896

This was a period of solid consolidation. At the end of each season, a member of the committee would summarise and analyse results. In the USA, the benchmark for an acceptable season is '500' or 50% wins and coaching jobs are lost or retained based on this figure. Over this particular period the First XV won 98, lost 85 and drew 26. This, on the whole, might be considered a positive outcome. Towards the end of this short period, the club secretary noted with pride:

"In these days we were a fair match for Bradford and all the leading clubs of the North."

During the 1888/9 season, the club organised a tour of Ireland and played against Dublin's prestigious Lansdowne club as well as Queen's College, Belfast, and the North of Ireland side. York, Cambridge Nomads and Old Millhillians were also among their opponents. A crowd of over 2,000 attended a friendly with Durham City in 1891. The scoring system remained complex with Durham City victorious by "one try and six minors to four minors".

Perhaps the most interesting aspect of the 1887-1896 period was the growing rivalry with another County Durham side - Hartlepool Rovers. Though formed six years after Sunderland, the Hartlepool side had quickly made a name for itself by producing international players, hosting the visiting Maori side in 1888 and taking part in the first ever Barbarians match. The annual tussle between Sunderland and Rovers took on a particular meaning as all the proceeds went to a Hartlepool hospital and the event attracted a large crowd.

This period also saw the decline and fall of junior clubs playing close to the Sunderland rugby ground. Humbledon, Sunderland Rangers and Sunderland Rovers all failed to survive the 1880s leaving Sunderland RFC as the only club in town until Sunderland Nomads was formed in 1892. Perhaps the growing popularity of the association game in the town had something to do with this. The success of the small mining village team at Tudhoe in Durham was also a sign of the times. This team attracted miners and was responsible for knocking Sunderland out of the County Cup in 1891. The score in the game was two goals and two tries to one penalty goal and two tries.

2.5: A Sunderland RFC side c.1886/7

1897 - 1907

For a variety of reasons, which should become clear as the chapter progresses, these may be considered the most successful years in the club's history. In *TAAB,* they were accorded the title 'The Elliot Years' and rightly so. Sunderland-born and Wellington College educated Edgar 'Tegger' Elliot was the glue which bonded together the club and county sides and, for one season, the international side too. He was a vastly talented sportsman (see Appendix Three) and at his best as a dashing winger. Closely matched by fellow club, county and international back Norman Cox, Elliot was the talk of the club from the minute he made his teenage appearance in the 2nd XV in

1896 until his departure for South America in 1907 (he did, however, miss one season while serving with the armed forces in South Africa). During the Elliot years, the club regularly fielded three sides and had a strong fixture list. It also seems to have attracted players from outside the town.

2.6: Edgar Elliot in a Durham County side

With another successful County Cup under the belt (see below), the club continued to make steady progress with its regular fixtures as shown by the results of the 1st XV for the 1896/7 season. The side won over half of their matches and lost in the final of the County Cup. In one of the first seasons where points counted they amassed 155 and conceded 97. There were convincing victories over Durham School and University and big losses to well-organised village side Tudhoe, and West Hartlepool. The secretary was fulsome in his praise of the 1st XV in his annual reports and success seemed to have increased the zeal of the committee. A new chairman and secretary in 1905 set out between them a clear system of sub-committees and duties.

The contributions of the 2nd and 3rd XVs to the club during this period make for interesting and, at times amusing, reading. At one point the 2nds appeared strong - at another, woefully weak. In 1897, for example, they lost a cup-tie to the village side of Hamsteels. Only eleven players turned up; two of these were lost to injury during the game and Hamsteels piled on the points. The secretary put the general failure down to the number of players needing to be used across the season. They kept on coming "like the parade of ghosts in Macbeth", he wrote.

The same secretary noted that things had gone "from bad to worse" by the end of the 1897/8 season. The 2nd XV had managed only 37 points for and had 202 points against. A match had not been won since 22 November and two fixtures had been broken - a disgraceful record for which there were "no excuses". He also spelt out the reasons for this - reasons which may be familiar to many a modern selector. Players in this side turned up to play just as it suited them. They didn't "answer their cards" until the last minute and those who were asked to replace them often refused "on the score of injured dignity" (viz., "I see I'm good enough to play for you now!"). Some were known to have stood down from an away match on "a paltry excuse" and were then seen watching the 1st XV's home game. The committee had had enough and cancelled all the 2nd XV fixtures for the following season.

At the beginning of the following season a group of humbled young players appeared before the committee to appeal for the reintroduction of the 2nd XV. This was duly done and the club was rewarded by improved performances. The boot then appears to have been on the other foot, with Hartlepool Old Boys 2nd XV derided in 1899 for "not turning up". The same XV failed to appear in the next season, reported as "defunct".

Reading between the lines, the 3rd XV, when it did play, was more like a modern colts' side. In January 1905, it took on Newcastle Royal Grammar School, one of the region's premier school sides. Like the Seconds, the 3rd XV wobbled from time to time and there was some discussion of discontinuing fixtures at the end of the 1907/8 season.

Unfortunately, the results for this period are incomplete but those for the earlier part of the period (1897 – 1903) seem to indicate around the '500' mark with the 1st XV recording 80 wins and 81 losses against increasingly tough opposition. The average score during this period was worked out as approximately 8-7 in Sunderland's favour.

1907 - 1914

The final section of the pre-war period is seen as less glamorous than the one preceding it. Norman Cox retired from the game in 1905 and Tegger Elliot left the country in 1907. As other senior players faded, it was left to a generation of youngsters to learn the game the hard way. They appeared to be gelling as a side when the 1914/15 season was abandoned due to the outbreak of war.

All these periods, and indeed the years up to the end of the Second World War, are covered in a delightful handwritten memoir by R Curry which is in the Local Studies Library. His views on the club and players will turn up from now onwards and make for fascinating reading. Up until the mid 1890s, like many Sunderland folk, he had little interest in rugby and was "deep in association football at Newcastle Road".

As an interesting footnote, where records do exist, they reveal that the 1st XV played an average of 25 games a season. The number of games played per season was then to rise rapidly in the twentieth century eventually reaching between thirty and forty.

2.7: 1912 First XV with Charles Pickersgill, front row, hands crossed

The Players

As in the early years of the club, families continued to play a major role. In the wider sports club it was reckoned that some 28 families were providing around 200 sportsmen soon after the move to Ashbrooke. Edgar 'Tegger' Elliot was the nephew of William and international Charles. His brother Henry (Harry), considered by some to be as good as Edgar, played for a single season while on a break from a new life in America. Norman Cox was the brother of county player Burdon. New names also entered the frame – Burn (Charles b. 1868, Alleyne b. 1869 and Donald b. 1874), Featherstonehaugh (Albany b. 1876 and Edward b. 1877) and the Crow brothers, Tom (b. 1868) and Dick (b. 1871). The Crows were a pair of fliers who played for other local clubs as well. A second family of Thompsons also emerged - the sons of Robert Thompson, a major shipbuilder in the town and described in the 1881 Census as "head of the firm of J L Thompson".

Among the individuals, William Bell was one of the great club characters. He fought to prevent the move to the association game and was reckoned to be man of the match while on loan to Hartlepool Rovers for their game against the Maoris in 1888. He had a reputation for his fierce tackling from full back and was said to be responsible for limiting the New Zealand visitors to a very narrow victory. He played representative rugby and in later life became a much-respected sports administrator. He was President of Durham RFU for five years and served as the County Representative on the RFU for another five. He appears on numerous team photographs of later years because of his key administrative role. Ironically he later became heavily involved in the administration side at Sunderland AFC.

The vast majority of the players were still from the upper-middle class. William Bell was a solicitor, the Featherstonehaugh family was prominent in the glass industry, the Crows were town centre auctioneers and lived in a house right next to the one in which Charles Alcock was born. The Burn boys were sons of a wealthy engineer. Nearly all of them lived near the Ashbrooke ground, which explains the rationale behind the club's move there. In the mid 1890s, some of the players had telephones and their numbers show how rare this was - the Thompsons' telephone number was 13, the Laings' 16 and tricky centre and shipowner Jenneson Taylor's 22.

The majority of youngsters who began to take over just before the First World War came from similar families and were shipbuilders, shipowners or shipbrokers. This was true of the Pickersgills (Charles, Edgar and Frank), Preston Horan and Robert Bartram, Young Vauxes also began to appear in both the 1st XV and 2nd XV. The name of Vaux was associated with town centre business and, in particular, with brewing and the production of ales such as Double Maxim - thus named because of the family's military connections.

A faded photograph of a 2nd XV of the late 1880s/early 1890s has survived with the names of players inscribed on the back. It features a young Tom Crow and Alleyne Burn, which would suggest that it was taken just before or just after the move to Ashbrooke. Interestingly there seems to be a little more of a social mix in this side with Thomas Eggleston (b. c.1864), Robert Rowntree (b. c.1869) and Charles Francis (b. c.1866) all the sons of shopkeepers. James Corder, son of a wealthy grocer and living a stone's throw from the ground, later became one of the town's eminent local historians. His Corder Manuscripts are among the most valued of collections in the city's local studies library. Leonard Iliff (b. c.1867) was a solicitor's clerk in his teens.

2.8: Faded 2nd XV picture c.1886/7

Although difficult to prove, it is noteworthy that the names of those who progressed to the First XV and county were among the elite of the town. This may be doing them an injustice and their promotion may well have been based on skill alone.

The County Cup

The First XV played in a single cup final during its early years. Between 1887 and 1914, it featured in three - 1897, 1903 and 1904. The first final was lost 12-0 to old rivals Hartlepool Rovers and, according to the club's annual report, the opponents deserved their success - with reservations:

"On the day's play last Saturday, the Hartlepool Rovers were fairly entitled to their victory, still the result was by no means a foregone conclusion and was no doubt aided by a piece of luck in their winning the toss with a strong wind, and in one of our forwards being disabled early in the game."

The loss came despite three training sessions in the week before the game and a stirring speech on the Friday night from old campaigner William Bell.

In 1903, the other senior side from the Hartlepools, West Hartlepool, was defeated in the final by 8-5. The victorious side must have been one of the most talented put out by the club in its history. Norman Cox and Tegger Elliot were both internationals. Tegger's brother Henry, on a year's break from work abroad, was a Barbarian. Alan Ayre Smith, a doctor, had played for an early British Lions' side, and Phil Clarkson had made a big mark on English rugby at county level (see below).

The club reported succinctly that the 1st XV:

"…won the Durham Senior Cup for the first time for the last 21 years. The success was greatly due to the excellent captaincy of George Rhind and in honour of which a dinner was held at the Grand Hotel, Sunderland."

In the following year, the 1st XV made the final once again only for West Hartlepool to gain revenge by 9-3. The secretary noted:

"The First Fifteen met West Hartlepool in the Final Round of the Durham Senior Cup when a big effort was made to retain the trophy but after a hard-fought game our opponents proved successful."

2.9: An Edwardian 1st XV outside the new pavilion

There are few other references to the County Cup in club records, except for details of a massive row with the County Union over a cup match with village side Hamsteels. The details of the row are of little interest but at some point the integrity of the Sunderland committee was challenged and this led to a considerable amount of vitriolic correspondence. At one point it seemed that the club would take the matter to the RFU but, in the end, things were sorted out in a fairly amicable way.

By the time the club was at Ashbrooke, junior clubs had begun to play for a County Cup. The Sunderland 3rd XV eventually began to participate in the competition but did not enjoy success until well into the twentieth century.

The Committee

The relative success of a rugby club is often dependent on the quality of its organisation and it is interesting to reflect on the make-up of the committee around the turn of the century. Thanks to the Census of 1901 and the wonderful search engine provided by *The Genealogist* web site it has been possible to discover much about the 12 men who then formed that committee.

In 1901, the oldest committee member was 36 and the youngest 22. Club captain Norman Cox (23), County representative Charles Burn (33) and secretary Jenneson Taylor (25) all held posts. George Wreford Brown (26) was a minister of the church, born at rugby-playing Clifton near Bristol, New York-born George Rhind (also 26) was living with his relatives, the ship-owning Bartrams and training to be a draughtsman. He was captain of the successful cup-winning side of 1903. David Todd (36) was an Irish-born physician and surgeon. Tegger Elliot was the 22 year old. The remainder included a shipowner, a medical student, a solicitor and an engineering merchant.

The addresses of the committee members were written down in copperplate handwriting in front of the minutes. As might be expected, nearly all were in the large terraces and semi-villas of the Ashbrooke suburb close to the ground. One was north of the river and two in the town centre but similar in style to those houses in Ashbrooke. The vast majority had cooks and housemaids as well as general domestics.

The committee was very similar in social structure to that of the earlier 1880s although the average age, at mid 20s, was slightly higher. In both cases there was a vast difference from the committee running the rugby club at the time this book was being written in 2011 - especially in terms of age!

County Rugby

If the results of the rugby club could be regarded as sound rather than spectacular during the period 1887 to 1914, the same could not be said of those of the Durham County side. According to the early county history, these were halcyon days and, on further reflection, probably the most successful in the history of Durham County rugby.

During the late nineteenth and early twentieth century, the annual County Championship (operative from the late 1880s) held a prestige, which has since been eroded. It was also an important step upon the road to the regional trials and national selection. The final took place between the champions of the north and the champions of the south and between 1899 and 1909, Durham County was utterly dominant in the north. It appeared as northern representatives in nine national finals, winning five and sharing one and contesting the crown of crowns with Gloucestershire, Devon, Cornwall and Kent.

Sunderland players played key roles in Durham's success at every stage. During the 1902/3 season, for example, six Sunderland players appeared for the county on a regular basis - a considerable contribution when the number of 'selectable' Durham clubs is taken into consideration. Tegger Elliot and Norman Cox were the lynchpins of the back division and Phil Clarkson (b. 1879; Sunderland 1900-1906, county 1903-1906) made a real name for himself at county level. In 1905, he became the first Englishman to cross the All Blacks' line to score a try.

The game between Durham and the New Zealand All Blacks was played at Hollow Drift - Durham City's home ground - in front of 8,000 spectators. Two Sunderland players were in the county side. Clarkson played in the backs and Cyril Stock in the forwards. This was the seventh game of the All Blacks' first tour to Europe and they had already played three clubs and three counties and recorded six victories. They had scored over 200 points with a four-point drop goal from Devon the only reply.

The Durham game was by far the toughest match with the final result 16-3. It got off to a bizarre start as two Durham players had missed the train and the full back had forgotten his boots and had to play in shoes. New Zealand scored two unconverted tries before the Durham pack began to dominate and a well-worked move got the ball out to one of the centres then to Clarkson on the wing. He was then able to score "the first try conceded by New Zealand on tour" (thus described in the official history). The crowd "went wild" although the conversion was missed leaving the score at half time a mere 6-3 to the visitors.

To place this narrow loss in context, the All Blacks thumped a joint Hartlepool and West Hartlepool side by 63-0 only four days later in front of a crowd of 13,000. The visitors only had 22 points scored against them in the entire tour - and Sunderland's Clarkson scored three of them!

Phil Clarkson came from East Boldon, a community under the influence of both South Shields (Westoe RFC) and Sunderland. He was the son of a gentleman shipowner and broker, and worked as a dealer in oils. He is instantly recognisable on team photographs and Curry recalls him as a player of courage and determination with a wonderful

2.10: Phil Clarkson in a Durham County side

sense of humour. He always had a "sly grin" and was ready for "badinage" with spectators. Stock was one of the players attracted to the club from outside. Darlington born, he was in the sixth form at rugby-playing Sedbergh School in 1901. He then played for Durham University and was part of the Sunderland 1st XV from 1903 to 1905.

Nathaniel Neilson was another Sunderland county player. He gave his life in the First World War (see Chapter Three). He played for the county against the visiting South Africans in 1906 and, by all accounts, was badly injured. Concerns for his long-term health however proved ill-founded although the injury may well have brought his playing career to an end.

The county was less successful during the periods before and after these halcyon days. Regulars during the earlier period (1887-1896) included William Bell, Burdon Cox, Tom and Dick Crow and the Burn brothers. The first county match at Ashbrooke took place ninth months after the ground opening - against Northumberland in February 1888. There were also games with Lancashire and Cheshire and the 3-0 victory over Cheshire was the first Durham County game in which points were awarded.

The years from 1910 to 1914 were described as Durham's 'famine years' - even in the Northern Championship. This mirrored Sunderland's lack of success during this period and the only Sunderland player featuring in the county side was the young Charles Pickersgill - a remarkable all-round sportsman (see Appendix Three).

An interesting aspect of county rugby during this period was the first appearance of the traditional four three-quarters in the backs during the 1890/1 season. Three of the four, Bell and the two Crow brothers, had Sunderland links.

The Representatives

During the 1887-1914 period, four players with strong Sunderland RFC connections featured in England sides. Two are already familiar, two less so.

The first of the two 'less familiar' characters is Francis Oswald Poole (b. 1870/1). The son of a clergyman, he was born at East Rainton - between Sunderland and the City of Durham. By 1881, he was living with his parents in Cheltenham. Between 1887 and 1889, still a teenager, he was featuring in the Sunderland First XV. He then moved on to Oxford University where he gained three caps, playing in all the home internationals during the 1895 season (Wales, Ireland and Scotland). In 1896 he again featured in the Sunderland side with the authors of *TAAB* noting that "the Reverend F O Poole appeared in the pack having obtained his international caps in the previous season". This reveals both his position in the field and his occupation.

2.11: F O Poole (back row, dark hair, on left arm of official) Durham County, 1895

Howard Marshall (b. 1870) was raised in a grand terrace less than ten minutes' walk from the Ashbrooke ground. He was the son of a Sunderland shipbuilder and shipowner and his name appears in Sunderland 1st XV sides from 1886 to 1890. He thus played in the same team as Poole - two teenagers and future internationals. By then Marshall was studying medicine at Cambridge after attending Barnard Castle School (then an association school despite its wonderful reputation for rugby in the late twentieth century). He appeared among the backs for the university although he was never awarded a blue.

Marshall has proved to be one of the most interesting characters in late nineteenth century rugby. In fact, the most detailed coverage of his life - and it is quite extensive - is on a French website. He had a number of claims to rugby fame, the biggest of which was the scoring of a hat trick of tries against the Welsh in Cardiff on his only international appearance.

The 1893 match between Wales and England has gone down as a classic. It was played in poor conditions. Hundreds of braziers had been placed on the pitch to keep off the frost and these had left burn marks. There was also a strong wind. England quickly took the lead with two tries and a conversion. Marshall scored one of the tries. The Welsh came back with two tries and a conversion only for Marshall to score another try, then one more. The Welsh replied with a penalty and a drop goal. The crowd was confused as the international points system was different from the other new one leaving the final score 12 –11 in Wales' favour. It gained Wales its first Triple Crown and the players were carried off the field on the shoulders of fans. The controversial Arthur Gould of 'The Gould Case' scored two of the three Welsh tries. Perhaps that's why admirers brought him the house.

Marshall's second claim to fame is that he is now recognised as one of the first British Lions. This was due to his selection to go to South Africa during the 1891/2 season with H E Maclagan's side. The Lions played 17 regional and invitational sides and three test matches. Marshall featured in 11 games including two tests. In the tests he was partnered in the backs by two fellow medics - future England captain Arthur Rotherham and Yorkshireman Edward Bromet. The Lions were victorious in both tests and Marshall scored seven tries and a drop goal during the tour. Although South Africa did not exist as a country at the time, the representative side in the three tests has since been recognised as South Africa. The famous politicians Rhodes and Kruger sponsored the entire tour.

Marshall's third claim to fame is that he was part of the early Barbarians side. He played his later club rugby for Blackheath and Richmond and it was while he was at the former that fellow player Carpmael devised the Barbarian concept. Marshall was included in the first Barbarians tour and scored the first Barbarian try in Wales. He was also on the Barbarians' organisational committee.

BARBARIANS v. DEVONSHIRE, AT EXETER, APRIL 1ST, 1891.
Back row.—G. Young, T. Whittaker, W. P. Carpmael, R. L. Aston, R. T. Duncan, P. F. Hancock, W. H. Manfield.
Middle row.—E. Emley, C. B. Nicholl, P. Christopherson, A. E. Stoddart, D. W. Evans, P. Maud.
Front row.—H. Marshall, C. A. Hooper, F. H. Fox, C. J. Vernon.

2.12: *Marshall as an early Barbarian (1891), clasping knee front left*

Marshall played in trial matches for the South against the North in 1891 and 1893. He also captained Blackheath and scored four tries for London versus the Combined Universities. His medical career took him to London, Nottingham and Gloucestershire. During the First World War he was in charge of a Red Cross Hospital and was awarded a CBE for his war work. He died at Westminster in October 1929 at the age of 59. His rugby career appears to have been cut short by serious injury. His brother Howard was a staunch cricketer and Ashbrooke member and administrator for most of his adult life.

Sunderland's other two international rugby players have already featured frequently in this chapter. Tegger Elliot played in all three home internationals (Wales, Ireland and Scotland) in the 1901 season and against Wales in 1904. He was also a reserve in other internationals. It is a sign of his greatness as an all-round sportsman that his entry in *TAAB* is in the cricket section. This is what the authors noted about his rugby:

"His greatest achievements in Rugby football were concentrated into a short(er) period, 1896-1903, during which he played 29 matches for the county including two Championship finals, scoring twenty tries and three goals. Originally a right wing threequarters, his reputation was gained on the opposing flank."

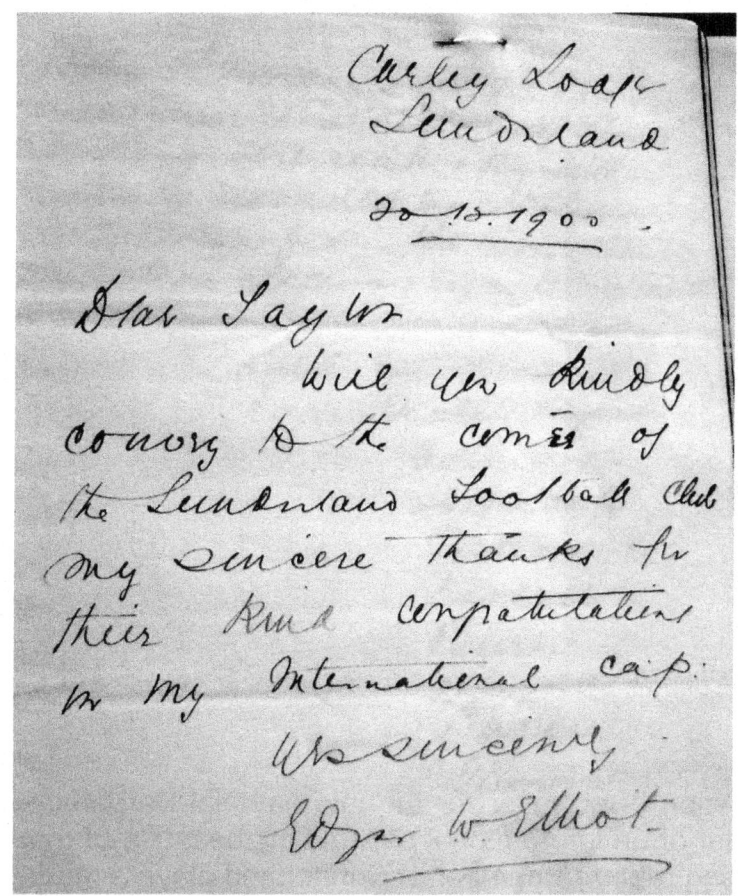

2.13: Edgar Elliot thanks the club for selection congratulations

Norman Cox was also in the backs with Elliot in the 1901 game against Scotland - a great moment for the club. The international recognition of both players was recorded in the club minutes and it is of interest to note that both men, though only in their early twenties, were on the club committee at the time their caps were awarded. In fact Cox was chairman and had to sign off the minutes containing his own congratulatory note. He was a natural centre who could play on the wing and played in 28 County Championship matches including five finals. He was a club official after retiring from playing and Curry remembered him as determined and fearless as a player with a good defence and an eye to opposition weakness.

2.14: Norman Cox in County Durham kit

To many lovers of rugby, selection of a player for the international Barbarians side carries a kudos rivalling that of an international call, mainly because of that side's stated dedication to running rugby. A number of Sunderland players made appearances for the Barbarians during the period. Poole, the rugby-playing reverend, played seven times for the Barbarians between 1892 and 1895 and Marshall appeared three times during the 1891/2 season. Tegger Elliot turned out nine times between 1901 and 1904. In 1903 his brother Henry (Harry) partnered him on two occasions before returning to work abroad. Two years earlier Norman Cox had been Tegger's partner - also on two occasions. Tom Crow also made two appearances in 1891/2 season, as did Tom Parker. There is a photograph of the 1891 Barbarians with the two Sunderland players seated side by side at the front. Crow's name appears on the programme for the very first Barbarians' match, guesting for Hartlepool Rovers. In one copy however, his name has been scratched out and replaced by another's so it would seem that he did not actually play.

Thomas Parker (b. 1867) is an interesting character - and instantly recognisable in photographs from what looks like a mass of blonde hair. He attended Durham School and Oxford University where he was awarded a rugby blue (as was Poole). He played for Sunderland in his youth - both before and after the move to Ashbrooke. He later played for Richmond where he had a trial for the South against the North in 1892. His father was a shipowner among other things and lived in the Ashbrooke area.

As might be expected, a number of other club players also featured in the regional international trials. Marshall, Tegger Elliot and Norman Cox certainly did. According to the authors of *TAAB*, "R N (later Sir Norman) Thompson was invited to play for the north on two occasions but declined owing to injury". His name crops up on Sunderland RFC team sheets between 1896 and 1898 and he was from the well-known Thompson shipbuilding family. Norman Cox's elder brother Burdon had a trial in 1888 with William Bell following in 1890 and Phil Clarkson in 1905. All three have already featured in this chapter.

Another Sunderland player to have his name raised into the limelight in recent years is Alan Ayre Smith (b. 1876). In times past, he was recognised simply as an excellent player who put his occupation as a doctor before his sport. His chances of a cap were lost when he decided to help out on the medical side during the Boer War. However, a foreign tour in which he took part has recently been recognised as a key one in the development of rugby. This is what is now regarded as the first British Lions' tour to Australia in 1899. There were 20 games on this tour. Ayre Smith played in 17 including the four now classified as tests. He scored a try in the Lions' victorious second test. He studied at Durham University and Guys Hospital and returned to Sunderland to play in and captain the 1st XV during the early twentieth century. His father, a surgeon, lived in the Ashbrooke area although Alan was brought up in the family home in Yorkshire and in London.

Conclusion

As the title of the chapter suggests, 1887-1914 was a period for doubts and decisions. Within the wider framework of British sport, Sunderland RFC had looked at the alternatives of professionalism and association football and had rejected both. By the end of the Edwardian era (1910), the club was settling into the role it was to maintain for most of the twentieth century - that of a typical English amateur rugby union club. In many rugby clubs, there was a kind of veiled professionalism. There are no signs of this at Sunderland RFC - or even hints. Both the rugby club and the overarching general club seemed to be limping from financial crisis to financial crisis with little income and it doesn't appear to have been because they were paying rugby players 'under the table'. In any case the governing board (see Appendix One) remained staunchly in favour of amateur sport. The rugby club was thus to play mainly in friendlies and County Cups and to be judged by its fixture list and results against traditional local rivals.

Against this background, it is possible to reflect positively on the first forty-odd years of the club's existence. Here was a club with a far from insignificant role to play in the early development of the game as a popular sport in England. The side which turned out in the 1889/90 season was captained by an international and Barbarian and featured two other future internationals (one a Barbarian), as well as two England trialists and another Barbarian. This is a record of which the club can be justifiably proud.

Chapter Three
Wars Intervene - Playing 'A Game More Grim' (1914-1945)

In the history of Durham County rugby published in 1936, the authors suggest that, some twenty years earlier, local players had gone off to play "a game more grim". At county level, seven of the squad for the 1913/14 season gave their lives in the 1914-18 conflict and ten Hartlepool Rovers players with county connections failed to survive the war. Sunderland RFC also gains a reference in Tony Collins' recent history of rugby because of the large number of members volunteering for active service within a few days of hostilities breaking out.

During the thirty-plus years between 1914 and 1945, a third of the time was taken up with war; two thirds were not. Inevitably the war years had a huge effect on the game of rugby but in what follows, the years of peace are given appropriate coverage.

Leaving the war years (1914-1918 and 1939-1945) aside for a moment, it could be argued that little changed in the way that rugby union was played over the remainder of this lengthy period. The game had been robbed of many of its players by 1919 and adjustments had to be made; otherwise club rugby consisted mainly of friendlies and County Cup games often supported by merit tables compiled by the local press. Clubs continued to be judged by the strength of their fixture lists and County Cups were still held in high esteem.

At a higher level, the game was being brought to a wider public with the introduction of the wireless and the development of cinema newsreel. The structure of international trials changed and touring sides from abroad continued to be greeted with great enthusiasm. The Home Internationals became the Five Nations with the addition of France in 1910 (although the arrangement did not prove permanent). This has had little effect on the history of Sunderland RFC as it took place a few years after the final peacetime international appearance by a Sunderland player.

It was during these inter-war years that Sunderland RFC became 'one among many'. Gone were the days of producing internationals and trophy-winning county players. Instead the club settled down to provide weekly entertainment and exercise for large numbers of local men. It did not create waves on the national rugby scene although it remained conscious of its history and constantly aware of its regional standing. From the club minutes and newspaper reports, it is also clear that this was a period when the performance of all sides - 1st XV, 2nd XV and 3rd XV - came to be treated with equal respect and interest.

Fixtures and Funding

As with many other clubs, the club's strength and weakness continued to be judged by the quality of its fixture list. Overall, the club's standing in the world of rugby declined slightly during this period - particularly in the 1920s - and, with respect to the opposition, the quality of the fixture list was often not what it had been in Victorian and Edwardian times. On occasions, efforts to restore old rivalries met with failure but every now and then there were successes, and this is the way rugby union seems to have worked at this level.

On a number of occasions, and particularly after a good season for the 1st XV, the committee made positive efforts to improve its fixture list, determined "to seek more attractive fixtures" and to "endeavour to obtain a few attractive fixtures with more distant clubs". Links were set up with well-respected sides in Scotland including Gala, Edinburgh Wanderers, Watsonians and Jedforest. A long relationship with Manchester-based Heaton Moor also began and games with Harrogate O.B. in Yorkshire were set up. The latter fixture created an interesting problem as Harrogate is one of the few sides to have a similar rugby top to Sunderland's and Sunderland had to borrow the county shirts for one of their Harrogate fixtures.

The influence of former player Alan Bean was also to be seen in the late 1930s as he became a top referee while still Fixtures' Secretary for the club (in 1939 he refereed an England Trial at Twickenham). Thanks to him, touring sides such as the Oxford Greyhounds and the University Vandals dropped into Ashbrooke. As war approached, the RAF base at nearby Usworth set up a side which enjoyed regular fixtures against Sunderland 2nd XV.

It is also interesting to note how important funding was as an element in fixture arrangement. The annual Boxing Day game against Durham City was played on a shared gate agreement in the late 1930s as was a hastily arranged away match with Westoe (in the Westoe case after expenses had been deducted). In 1930 rail fares were paid and a tea provided for visiting Watsonians. Jedforest offered £5 in return for a 1st XV fixture in Scotland. The Sunderland committee asked for and got £2 and a share in the gate. When distance was involved 'fares' and 'teas' appear to have been the very bottom line.

Raising the money to pay for this was another key element. In January 1931, members were charged 1/- (one shilling) to watch a first round County Cup tie and non-members 1/6 (one shilling and sixpence) for 'ringside seats'. When the Old Leysians visited on a tour game, non-members were charged 6d (sixpence) and members had to pay to use the stand. Tickets were sold for the Watsonians' clashes. Around the same time a dispute arose over the number of free tickets the county expected clubs to hand out to visiting team for cup-ties. Wearing his county hat, Sunderland man Eric Watt Moses dealt with the matter wisely, suggesting that the clubs should sort it out among themselves in each individual case.

There are also signs that the club remained staunchly amateur during this period. In the mid-1930s players were asked to contribute 6d a week to a travelling fund. In 1937, a rule was passed that allowed players three games' leeway before paying 'subs'. After that it was a case of 'no pay, no play'.

Better fixtures required a more dedicated approach from players and also held up the prospect of larger crowds. Training was firmly fixed to Tuesdays and Thursdays and lighting introduced for these sessions. As war approached, this lighting came to be operated by electricity. Attractive 1st XV fixtures were advertised round the town on sandwich boards and a large batch of blank advertising posters purchased. In the early 1920s, efforts were also made to rouse more public interest as matches came to be advertised in the local newspapers, the theatre and at the cinema.

It was somewhat ironic that the fixture list proposed for the 1940/1 season looked extremely attractive - thanks mainly to the efforts of Alan Bean. In the late 1930s, the 1st XV enjoyed a run of good results and saw its captain made captain of the county - and then war broke out.

Pitches and Other Matters

It was during this period too that problems with the pitch began to emerge. Ashbrooke lies on the top of old mine workings and it became increasingly clear that the underground foundations of 1887 were less than satisfactory. Ship ballast and general rubbish had been used and any drains there had become clogged making general drainage poor. As a result careful work on the main pitch was necessary then, and has been necessary ever since.

In the early 1930s, the question of a second pitch surfaced once more but nothing was done about it. This remained (and to some extent still remains) a major problem.

Other little titbits may strike a familiar chord today. Younger members of the club complained about the cost of membership and match fees and eventually a reduced fee was agreed for a limited number of youngsters. Towards the outbreak of war, common start times were also formalised by the county. These moved between 2:45 and 3:15 dependent upon the time of year.

In general, the club minutes during this period are fairly thin - especially in the 1920s. In most cases, they consist of lists of the names of those chosen to play in the three XVs. They do, however, point to one or two interesting developments. In September 1922, the committee decided to put numbers on 1st XV players for the first time. Each member of the squad was given a number running from three to eighteen. Numbers one and two were not given out. Programmes were also printed and published for 1st XV fixtures. At the beginning of the 1922/3 season, the *Echo* correspondent proudly noted that the club had fielded four sides for the first time in his recollection.

Merit Tables

Soon after the First World War, the rugby committee rejected the idea of joining a league but pressure came on both the 1st XV and 2nd XV via the merit tables published in the local paper. The table was made up of senior clubs in Durham and Northumberland and positions allotted based on the percentage of games won. Only games played between merit table sides counted. At one point in the early 1920s, there were nineteen sides in the table. All are still playing in one form another and it is interesting to list them and to note where they were in the league system during the 2010/11 season.

Durham Clubs

Sunderland - Level 7
Westoe - Level 4
Hartlepool Rovers - Level 6
West Hartlepool - Level 6
Hartlepool Old Boys (Hartlepool today) - Level 8
Gateshead Fell (now Gateshead) - Level 7
Winlaton Vulcans - Level 8

Ryton - Level 7
Durham City - Level 6
North Durham (merged with Gateshead - Level 7)

Northumberland Clubs

Gosforth Nomads (Gosforth newly constituted - Level 7)
Tynedale - Level 3
Medicals - Level 7
Northern - Level 6
Blaydon - Level 3
Old Novos (Novos today) - Level 7
Percy Park - Level 6
Armstrong College (Newcastle University today) - in University/College system

As today, Blaydon and Tynedale were strong sides in the 1920s. In the 1921/2 season Sunderland 1st XV finished 14th out of 19 in the table. The 2nd XV, playing mostly against other 2nd XVs, ended up 10th out of 28 sides.

Anatomy of a Season - 1924/5

The club was still about families. One of them was named Greig and Donald Greig, a great enthusiast, as will be seen, kept a scrapbook relating to the rugby club during the early 1920s. Filled with newspaper cuttings of match reports and midweek summaries, it allows us to look at how the club was doing in one season soon after the First World War.

This season came on the back of one considered successful for the 1st XV. As the idea of a league was once more discussed and rejected, it is safe to assume that the club was now no longer involved in a league system. During this season, the All Blacks trained at Ashbrooke prior to their game against Durham County at Sunderland AFC's Roker Park (see below) and one of the senior players was heard to declare that Ashbrooke was "a proper rugger ground".

During the season, the club was able to put out three XVs on a regular basis, named 1st, 'A' and 'B'. The 1st XV had 31 friendly fixtures as well as games in the County Cup. All the fixtures were in the north-east of England and, at this time, included strong sides such as Hartlepool Rovers, Durham City and Gosforth. The 'A' and 'B' seasons were slightly shorter although these teams too now had their County Cups.

The season was a mixed one for the 1st XV. By now the local *Sunderland Echo* had developed a kind of mascot in the form of a cartoon rugby ball with a face. The character thus developed either smiled or grimaced according to the result, thus giving the reader advanced warning of what to expect. Over the season, the mascot grimaced as often as it smiled.

3.1: The Echo ball heralds bad news

A decent home win against a Hartlepool Rovers side weakened by county calls was offset by a heavy defeat in the away fixture with the county players back in the Rovers' side. Both Gosforth and Blaydon were defeated home and away although Durham club Ryton proved a thorn in the side both in the regular season and in the very first round of the County Cup. The 'A' XV had a solid regular season and ended it on a high by taking the 2nd XVs' County Cup.

Reading through the newspaper accounts of games gives some idea as to the leading players of the day and in 1924/5, three in particular stand out. Jack Moncaster, a county player, was mentioned frequently in press reports. After his death, his nephew sent some photographs and memorabilia to the club and these now form part of the Ashbrooke archive.

E L 'Lorry' Squance was the 1st XV's premier place kicker and a real character who also enjoyed considerable success as a cricketer. Henry Clayton Greene was perhaps the most talented player in the club and his presence was sorely missed during the early part of the season. He broke his collarbone in a county trial match. He learnt his rugby at Durham School but headed south thereafter and played for Blackheath and Kent before returning to his native Sunderland.

If the club's general reputation continued to be high, it was due to the organisation of its officials. Charles Pickersgill, influential all-round sportsman, was club and county chairman and worked tirelessly towards making the All Blacks' game a success. A young Alan Bean was club secretary. In years to come he was to make a considerable mark in the world of national and international rugby refereeing.

After a series of 1st XV losses early in the season, supporters agreed universally that there had "never been such incompetent tackling in the entire history of the club". This is a complaint, which reared its head at earlier times and has re-surfaced on numerous occasions since!

County Cups

As noted earlier, these were years in which the achievements of all the club's sides were treated with equal interest and this was particularly true when it came to County Cups. By this time there was a competition at county level for 1st, 2nd and 3rd teams with the seconds and thirds playing the equivalent sides of senior clubs as well as the numerous junior clubs that were springing up (especially during the 1930s).

During the inter-war years, the 1st XV featured in three County Cup finals, winning two of them. In 1927, the final was lost 10-5 to Ryton. A programme for this match can be seen in the Hartley Elliott File in the club archives.

3.2: 1927 Durham Cup final
programme

In 1928, a 17-8 victory in the final against old rivals Durham City brought the cup back to Ashbrooke for the first time for almost quarter of a century. The Ashbrooke archive contains a wonderful colour cartoon of a happy smiling *Echo* ball hand in hand with cup-winning captain Roy Wilson.

ROY WALKS OFF WITH THE CUP.

3.3: A happy Roy Wilson and a happier Echo ball

Success was achieved again in 1931 with Durham City once more the opposition. The score was 14-9, and captain on the day Dr H J Nicholson. The team also made semi finals on four other occasions in the 1930s but lost heavily in each case - three times to Durham City and once to West Hartlepool. Sunderland scored only three points in the four matches (although, in fairness, the 1939 defeat by Durham City was in a replay after a scoreless draw).

The 2nd XV reached two finals during this period. The first, in 1925, ended in a narrow victory over Durham City by 9 points to 7. Robert Bartram captained the side that included future international referee and administrator Alan Bean. In 1934, the final was lost to West Hartlepool. As with the first team, a number of semi finals were reached in the 1930s resulting in narrow losses to Darlington, Hartlepool Rovers and Durham City.

Perhaps the most unfortunate side was the 3rd XV which made three finals and lost all three - to Hartlepool Boys' Brigade 1st XV (6-5 in 1922), to West Hartlepool 3rd XV (8-3 in 1928) and Throston Wanderers 1st XV (15-0 in 1931). Throston Wanderers was a Hartlepool junior side. Keeper of the scrapbook Donald Greig captained the Sunderland side on the first two occasions. He also scored all the points, The defeat in the 1932 final was the only one experienced by the 3rd XV in the entire 1931/2 season.

Sunderland was central to the playing of the County Cup in its early days. By 1923, over 50% of the County Cup finals played since 1881 had taken place on Sunderland's home pitch either at Ashbrooke or at Chester Road.

3.4: Cup match against Durham City in the 1920s

The Players

Over the twenty-year period, a number of interesting characters pulled on the Sunderland shirt. Some will feature prominently in the county and representative section, some in the section dedicated to the wars and some in both.

With three teams turning out on a regular basis, it is not surprising to find a number of loyal club servants requiring a mention. Three in particular were later to serve not only club and county in key official roles but also the whole game of rugby union. Future RFU president Eric Watt Moses had his club career disrupted by the First World War but returned to make 1st team appearances in the seasons that followed. He was brought up in a house overlooking the ground and he became a vital part of the club and county committee. His father was a solicitor and he followed in his footsteps. Future international referees Hartley Elliott and Alan Bean featured in various sides in the 1920s and, as noted above, Alan Bean was a tireless committeeman (all three have biographies in Appendix Two).

Charles Ranken (b. c.1894), full back just after the war, belonged to a rugby-playing family. His father was in the building and contracting business and lived within walking distance of Ashbrooke. Arthur Birchall (b. c.1887), who played in the 1919-20 season, was the son of a town centre confectioner. Thomas Booth (b. c.1898), player and club officer, was the son of a Wesleyan methodist minister from north of the river. Geoffrey Bryers, the son of a solicitor, was also from north of the river. The Pickersgill brothers (Charles and Edgar) lived in the Ashbrooke area. The Greig brothers were also local to the ground. Their father worked in the Post Office.

Although many of the leading lights of the club still belonged to the higher end of Sunderland society, some did not. An increasing number of players came from slightly humbler backgrounds although still regarded in their day as 'solid citizens'. Thus we have players who were involved in - or whose families were involved in - shopkeeping and clerical work and who inhabited the slightly smaller terraced houses on the Ashbrooke fringes.

County and Representative Players

During the inter-war years, many Sunderland players featured in the Durham County side although the side itself achieved relatively little in comparison to its Edwardian forebears. In the late 1920s, the county side lost all of its championship games across three seasons. It did, however, manage to make the County Championship final in 1932. This was played against Gloucestershire at Blaydon in front of a crowd of 12,000 with the visiting side ending up as victors. Only one Sunderland player was on the pitch that day - former Durham schoolboy W B Allan. He was a stalwart for the Sunderland 1st XV in the late 1920s and early 1930s and made twelve appearances in County Championship matches. It is estimated that some 150 county caps were awarded to Sunderland players between 1926 and 1936 and eight club players are known to have appeared for the county in the 1929/30 season.

3.5: W B Allan in Sunderland 1st XV

Second World War victim, Alan Spence, was also a county regular in the 1930s with fifteen County Championship appearances. He was arguably the best Sunderland player from this period and a first team player (except when injured) from 1928-1939. He was the only Sunderland player in the joint Northumberland/Durham side that took on the All Blacks during the 1935/6 season. It is indicative of the massive strength of these tourists that many of the clubs and counties found it necessary to combine to take them on during that tour. In consequence, the games were much tighter and by the time the All Blacks took on a joint Northumberland and Durham side in the eighth game of the tour at Gosforth in October 1935, they had already lost a close game to Swansea by 11-3. It is a sign of the quality of Alan Spence's play that he was selected in the forwards for the joint counties' side (this was after trials - the game was that important). A crowd of just fewer than 11,000 saw the tourists sneak home by 10-6 with both teams scoring two unconverted tries and a New Zealand drop goal making the difference. It was generally agreed that the counties' forwards had had the better of the visitors. Spence also played for the county against an International XV in the same season. The game took place at St Albans in Hertfordshire and had a twofold purpose; to raise awareness of rugby in a virtual rugby desert and to bring in funds for the distressed of Durham during a period of depression.

3.6: Alan Spence - a fine player and victim of war (Roy Wilson from the earlier cartoon in front)

Another Sunderland player of note at county level was future club administrator Arnold Dixon. He was the third generation Dixon to serve the wider club in one capacity or another and had played his rugby for Waterloo "with distinction" until returning to his native town in 1936. He then captained the club 1st XV as well as being the first Sunderland player to captain the county since Tegger Elliot in Edwardian times. In the years just prior to the Second War, Spence and Dixon were the only two Sunderland players to gain county caps.

3.7: A C Dixon in Sunderland's 1st XV

Other Sunderland players also served the county "with distinction across the period". Two of these - Jack Moncaster and Charles Pickersgill - have already been mentioned. According to press reports, Moncaster was a busy centre and, thanks to the generosity of his relatives, the club has pictures of him in action during a county trial and in a casual county side photograph. He made six appearances for the county in the 1920s.

3.8: Jack Moncaster while vice captain of Sunderland's 1st XV

Charles Pickersgill's name appears again and again in this book - as a rugby player, administrator and also as a multi-talented sportsman. This is what the authors of *To Ashbrooke and Beyond* wrote about him in relation to his rugby achievements:

"His rugby career was probably the longest of any member of the club for having secured his place in the XV as early as 1904 he gladly turned out in the late 'thirties to make up the 3rd XV in an emergency. His ten appearances as halfback embraced the period 1907-1919 and included the

County Championship final of 1913-14. He represented the club on the County Rugby Union from 1922 onwards, being its president from 1924-26 and much of the union's growth after the First World War is ascribable to his enthusiasm and drive."

As with Eric Watt Moses and many other Sunderland players, his career was interrupted by the First World War.

Other long serving county players included Geoffrey Cox, Morris Gelsthorpe, James Storey and Roy Wilson, all of whom are dealt with in the wars' section. H J Nicholson (12) and N C Marr (13) were other good county servants. H J Adams (8), E E Carruthers (6) J E Dobbie (5) and W F Macmillan (7) also played. The closest to taking another step up the ladder were John Dove, N C Marr and Henry Clayton Greene. Dove was a brewer's son who had two international trials - one for the North versus England and one for the Rest v England. He was a Sunderland forward in the years after the war. Clayton Greene (b. 1905) was another sporting all-rounder. He made seventeen county appearances and turned out for the Colours versus the Whites and the Possibles versus the Probables in 1939. His career was cut short by injury. N C Marr had two trials in 1933 both for the Possibles - once against the Probables and one against England. Older readers will be familiar with this rather strange way of trialling but the team names do, at least, give some indication of how close to a cap certain players came.

Special Matches

During the inter-war years there were a number of special matches in which the rugby club was heavily involved.

England Trial 1932

In March 1932, the club committee was pleased to receive a request from the RFU to be allowed to use Ashbrooke for the first of the England trial matches on 3 December of that year. The decision to comply with the request proved a good one as a crowd of 4,000 turned up to see what was, effectively, a full England side play against the Possibles. It was a close game, giving the selectors plenty of food for thought. West Countryman Tom Brown captained the England side, which also had the much-respected Plymouth player Eddie Richards at scrum half. Two players with Durham connections - Cliff Harrison and Carl Aardvold - also played.

County Diamond Jubilee 1936

As the authors of *To Ashbrooke And Beyond* proudly noted, "of the many stirring Rugby events at Ashbrooke, none aroused greater interest than the match played 26 September 1936". The game was between a Durham XV and an International XV and was played to mark the Diamond Jubilee of the County Union which had been established in the autumn of 1936. The International side was put together by legendary Hartlepool Rovers man, Bob Oakes. Oakes had been an England player and selector and was also a former president of the RFU. He had also played for the county on numerous occasions.

The team chosen by Oakes for this special occasion was packed with talented players and a large photograph of both sides has adorned the Ashbrooke pavilion for many years. There were thirteen international players in his team - six from England, two from Ireland, two from Wales and one from Scotland. The remaining four were Yorkshire county players. George Beamish of the RAF and Ireland captained the side and fittingly, in light of the occasion, Hospital, Services, University and Club sides were all represented.

3.9: County Jubilee match, 1936

There were a number of well-known players on view that day. The best known historically is 'Prince' Obolensky, arguably the most famous rugby player of all time - certainly prior to the professional era. In 1936 he was turning out for Oxford University and England and had made his mark in January of that year by scoring a wonder try for England against the All Blacks in a rare victory over the visitors. His family had fled the Russian Revolution of 1917 and 'The Prince' had just been made a British citizen. He was killed in a wartime flying accident at the age of 24.

H G 'Tuppy' Owen-Smith, a South African cricketer as well as an England rugby player, had already left his mark on Ashbrooke while playing his other sport. In 1929 as part of the touring South African side, he had scored a century and taken four wickets in five balls in a game against Durham County - including a hat trick. He played at full back for the International XV in the Jubilee Match.

At the tender age of 19, Haydn Tanner, the Welsh scrum half, was already the talk of the rugby world. During the previous year and while still at school, he had been instrumental in helping Swansea to victory over the All Blacks. His career continued after the Second World War and Tanner, who died in 2009, is regarded in some quarters as the finest scrum half ever.

The Durham side was a fairly strong one too. It contained two international players - Cliff Harrison of Hartlepool Rovers and England (and at one time England's oldest living player) and Alec McLaren of Durham City and Scotland. The other Durham sides represented were Darlington Railway Athletic, Westoe, Gateshead Fell, North Durham and Blaydon. Sunderland's single representative, as was often the case in the 1930s, was Alan Spence.

On a pleasant autumn day, the crowd of 6,000 was treated to a fine display of running rugby. The final score was 19-3 to the international side with its players crossing the opposition line on five occasions. Obolensky scored twice. The post-game celebrations were equally sumptuous with all the great and good of the game in attendance as well as numerous ex-Durham players. Perhaps the most interesting was W Hodgson of the defunct Tudhoe club. He had been the first miner to represent the county - in 1886.

Two other special matches in which Sunderland RFC was heavily involved took place away from Ashbrooke - at Sunderland AFC's Roker Park ground north of the river. On both occasions, the Ashbrooke rugby posts were used.

Durham County v All Blacks 1924

The game took place in October and was the tenth game in what was to prove a memorable tour. The visitors travelled all over Britain and also went to France and Canada. They were victorious in all their matches. There were one or two close games but the match against Durham was one of the thumpings with the final score 43-7 in the visitors' favour. The crowd of 15,000 was treated to a feast of tries (and also what the *Echo* reporter described as a 'weird dance' led by one of the Maori players). The official tour historian was kind enough, however, to record that Durham, one of the weakest of the counties at the time, was still rebuilding after the war. The only Sunderland player in the side was Dr Eccles. Alderson of Hartlepool Rovers and England scored all the Durham points. It was but slight consolation that a strong Yorkshire side lost 42-4 a few days later. The points built up against Durham (through ten tries) were the largest on the tour.

3.10: 1924 All Black photograph presented to the club

This game was a big success for Sunderland RFC which had been instrumental in its organisation. Ex-county player and all-round sportsman Charles Pickersgill was the Chairman of the club and the county. Prior to the match there was some concern that the visitors had to be guaranteed a sum of £200. After the match it was revealed that pre-sales alone came to £250 while a further £645 was taken at the gate. A later report suggested that some £200 still lay in county coffers after all the bills had been paid.

Durham and Northumberland v South Africa, 24 October 1931

Apart from the loan of the posts, this game has little place in the history of Sunderland RFC as there were no Sunderland players in the joint counties' side. The north-east side was convincingly beaten by 41 points to nil in front of a crowd of 17,000. Just under four years earlier, J E Dobbie of Sunderland had been in a joint counties' side that had taken on New South Wales Waratahs at Gosforth. The Waratahs won a thrilling contest 14-9, scoring the winning points in injury time. Dobbie is mentioned in match reports for his brave defence.

3.11: J E Dobbie in Sunderland's 1st XV

As noted above, the Ashbrooke posts were used at Sunderland AFC's ground for these games and during this period, relations between the professional football club, the rugby club and the Ashbrooke club in general seem to have been quite cordial. There were discussions at times about the possibility of the football club using Ashbrooke for training and cricket matches also took place between the footballers and Ashbrooke sides. This was particularly true in the 1930s at a time when Sunderland AFC won the FA Cup and star footballer Raich Carter was a keen and competent cricketer.

Wars Intervene

It has been difficult to get through this chapter without reference to the two great conflicts of the twentieth century. They put rugby careers on hold and, in too many cases, brought them to a sad and sudden close. Although club rugby as such was not operational for the ten years of conflict (1914-18 and 1939-1945), there was still relevant activity in and around the Sunderland club.

The First World War

As noted in the introduction to this chapter, Sunderland RFC's war effort has already attracted the interest of sports historians. More than forty members of the club joined up within days of war breaking out - a noteworthy event. This does not take account of those players, past and future, who were away at public school or university at the time or of those who became old enough to join up as the war progressed.

Naturally all club and representative rugby was brought to a halt for the duration of the war but the ground was still used for sport from time to time by garrison troops and by schools and youth groups. As was the case in many walks of life, women were instrumental in keeping the wider club going during this period.

The Second World War

As with the previous conflict, club and representative games were suspended although from time to time there were rugby matches set up and some, according to *TAAB*, were of a "notably high standard".

The ground itself also saw more wartime activity than it had done a quarter of a century earlier. Sunderland was a chief producer of the replacement ships for the merchant navy at this time. Famed for its rapid 'off-the-peg vessels' (many of which were produced in shipyards run by former players) the town and port was a popular target for enemy bombardment. The Ashbrooke area, though some distance from the shipyards, was hit quite badly and still bears the scars today. The ground itself and pavilion suffered bomb damage and there are thick files in the archives dealing with the financial compensation which took many years to sort out. All the records of junior club rugby, in the hands of Eric Watt Moses, were destroyed by enemy action.

Schools and youth groups continued to use Ashbrooke for sporting events but in general the condition of the playing surface deteriorated. Areas of the ground were turned over to allotments as part of the 'Dig for Victory' campaign and for some time Ashbrooke was occupied by a barrage balloon and those who looked after it. Club supporters were also heavily involved in the wartime 'Home Front' organisations that were springing up and it became increasingly difficult to find and to hold on to experienced ground staff.

A TRIBUTE
OF HONOUR
TO MEMBERS OF
ASHBROOKE CLUB
WHO SERVED IN
THE GREAT WARS
AND IN REMEMBRANCE
OF THOSE WHO LEFT
THESE PLAYING FIELDS
AND GAVE THEIR LIVES
IN THE FIGHT FOR
· · FREEDOM · ·
1914–1918 · 1939–1945

3.12: Ashbrooke Memorial Board

Players at War

This is a fairly lengthy section, which is in itself an indication of the effect of war on a 'typical' rugby club like Sunderland. Death, injury and the process of age robbed both club and players of years of sporting pleasure. Also, as was the wont with large industrial towns, Sunderland was close-knit and at the centre of the action. In the First World War, many Sunderland men joined the 7th Battalion of the Durham Light Infantry (DLI) which was part of the highly active 50th Division. Historically, Light Infantry Regiments, as the name suggests, were at the forefront in battle and suffered the consequences. The effect of the first day of the Somme on County Durham families, for example, has been written about on numerous occasions. Back on the rugby field it took four years before there were enough men to form a 2nd XV.

In the Second World War, Sunderland's own 125 Anti-Tank Regiment sailed into Singapore as it was being taken by the Japanese with consequences that are still felt in the modern city. The annual Remembrance Day Service, held a short distance from Ashbrooke, is claimed to be the second largest in the country.

The authors of *To Ashbrooke and Beyond* regarded the years from 1914 to 1918 as "wasted years". This is hardly surprising as only a handful of 1st XV players actively returned to the game. At least seven players lost their lives in the conflict. Nathaniel Neilson and George Carter had been part of the great Edwardian 1st XV and Neilson was a highly respected county player. He had been in the county side that took on the South Africans in 1906. He was a corporal in the Royal Fusiliers and was 30 years old when he was killed on the Front in February 1916. He is buried in France. Carter died the previous November. He was a second lieutenant in the Royal Artillery (RA) and his grave is in Bishopwearmouth Cemetery.

Andrew Legat and James Adamson were 1st XV representatives during the late Edwardian period. Legat, whose father was a surgeon, had played in the same side as his two brothers on a number of occasions. He was a second lieutenant in the Royal Field Artillery (RFA) when he fell in March 1917. Adamson was a captain in the same RFA and was killed on the Front two months later.

Edward Haydon Moore, Frederic(k) Longden and James Edwards were all in the 1st XV in the season before the war. Moore, who died on 27 March 1917, was a captain in the York and Lancaster Regiment. Former Durham schoolboy Longden was 30 years of age and a captain in the Durham Light Infantry (DLI).

He died in August 1918. Edwards was only 22 and a lieutenant in the DLI when he died in January 1917.

A number of those who played before the First World War gained awards for bravery as did some who returned to play after it. Robert Bartram, Geoffrey Hedley and Stanley Milburn, all lieutenants, were awarded Military Crosses. Captain Charles Potts and Majors 'Lorry' Squance and William Laing were too. Many of those named had played in the same side in the late Edwardian period and Potts had been captain of the 1st XV for a season.

Morris Gelsthorpe, a young man fresh out of Durham University, was mentioned in despatches and awarded a DSO (Distinguished Service Order). 'Gelly' as he was known to all and sundry is one of the most interesting characters to have played for the club and worth looking up on an internet search engine. Born in 1892, he reached the rank of lieutenant colonel during the war despite his youthfulness. While at Hatfield College, Durham prior to the war, he played rugby for Durham County. After the war, he entered the Church of England and became a curate in St Gabriel's parish not far from the Ashbrooke area. While in Sunderland, he served both rugby club and county and was part of the county side that won the Northern Group in 1920. After three seasons, he decided to follow one of his mentors and become a missionary. He went to Africa, became heavily involved in the Church Missionary Society and ended up as the Bishop of Sudan. He later returned to take over a parish in the south of England and died in 1968. There is a collection of his papers in the library at the University of Birmingham. While in Sunderland, he was a popular minister and was given a watch by the rugby club committee on his departure for Africa.

Dr Howard Marshall, who had played for the club as a teenager in the Chester Road days (and later scored a hat trick for England) was made a CBE for his work in running a Red Cross hospital. Promising pre-war youngster Preston Horan, an army captain, gained a Military medal and an MBE. Roy Wilson, captain of the 'high-flying' cup side of 1928, was awarded a Distinguished Flying Cross. William Gales entered the Order of the British Empire (OBE). Bartram, Horan and Laing were all from maritime families. The Squances were a well-known sporting family, which included doctors and accountants.

During the Second World War at least three rugby players from Sunderland RFC gave their lives. Alan Spence was the most prominent on the rugby field. He had been the club's long-serving and most successful representative player during the inter-war years. He was a sergeant observer in the RAF. Thomas Shacklock, a seagoing man from a maritime family, died while a chief engineer in the merchant navy. The Cox family, loyal rugby players and followers from Holmeside days, lost Rowland, a wing commander in the RAF. The wider Ashbrooke club lost even more members including, possibly, further rugby players who have not as yet been traced.

3.13: Thomas Shacklock in Sunderland kit

As in the First World War, a number of rugby players and former rugby players were rewarded for bravery. Pre-war county captain Arnold Dixon gained an MBE. Major James Storey was mentioned in despatches. He enjoyed a distinguished career for both club and county and played for the Territorial Army XV against the Army alongside clubmate W B Allan. Storey was a regular in the Sunderland First XV for most of the 1920s and 1930s and captained the side for a time in the early 1930s. Between 1929 and 1933, he made 20 appearances for the county including 17 Championship matches. Geoffrey Cox was awarded a British Empire Medal. He was the son of international Sunderland player Norman and nephew of Burdon Cox. Like his father, he played in the backs and was in the same club team as James Storey for many years. Between 1928 and 1935, he scored well over 400 points for the club including 101 points in the single 1930/31 season. He had developed his rugby skills at Rugby playing Loretto College in Scotland and was, according to the early county history, "a fine kicker off both feet". He made 15 appearances for the county bringing the Cox family total of county appearances to nearly 70. Other awards were made to G Fairclough, Alfred Bannister (Bronze Star USA) and Robert Cyril Thompson.

The greatest wartime honours, however, fell the way of a member of one of the club's founding families - Joe Kayll (b. 1914). A rugby player for Sunderland throughout the 1930s, Joe was one of the country's most prominent fighter aces with a wartime career that deserves a book in itself. His honours read DSO, OBE and DFC and a 'googling' of his name will flag up masses of fascinating details. To list but a few:

- In May 1940 his squadron brought down 32 enemy aircraft. Joe's personal tally was nine;
- He was actively involved in the Battle of Britain;
- A wing commander by the summer of 1941, his plane was brought down and he was captured;
- In 1942, he was part of a mass POW breakout and remained on the loose for a week before being recaptured;
- In Stalag Luft III, he was the escape officer and also responsible for security and intelligence among the prisoners. This was where the famous 'Wooden Horse' escape plan was carried out;
- His OBE came as a result of his escape efforts.

In later life, his main interest was in sailing. He was the grandson of Sunderland RFC's first international Henry Kayll and thus had five rugby-playing great uncles. His father, Major Kayll, was an active club official and administrator in the inter-war years. Joe Kayll died in 2000. Like a number of Sunderland rugby players, he was involved in the timber business. Stationed for some time at nearby Usworth in the 1930s, he took his place in the Ashbrooke side when his own station provided the opposition.

Other Inter-war Developments

Between 1914 and 1945, there were two other developments on the Sunderland rugby front worthy of note and it would be interesting to discover whether similar developments took place in other English clubs.

The first development came in the field of **'sevens' rugby.** The recent acceptance of the shortened form of the game as an Olympic sport has led to the misconception that this is a very modern game. This has been added to by its growth at an international level and by the television time afforded to it. Avid followers of the sport know otherwise and are aware of the Scottish Borders' role in the founding of sevens. It was introduced in 1883, ten years after the establishment of the Sunderland Club, and the first competition was held in Melrose, a couple of hours' drive to the north of Wearside.

Northumberland clubs were involved in sevens from the early days but it was in the inter-war years that the game really began to take off. The Middlesex Sevens have been going since the 1920s but the Sunderland club minutes do not reveal a real interest until much later. During the 1931/2 season, there was a spate of invitations to sevens' competitions on both sides of the border. The club committee politely declined the offers. Gala repeated the invitation towards the end of the following season but this was also declined. In this instance the reason given was the prospect of the club's appearance in County Cup finals around the same date as the festival.

In March 1932, a meeting of Durham junior clubs led to the establishment of an Easter 7s. The committee decided to send a representative side drawn from the 3rd XV and also offered to provide one of the match balls for the tournament. Towards the end of the following season, club and county regular James Storey agreed to take a sevens' side to the Middlesbrough 7s at Easter. At the same time, the 3rd XV side returned to take part in the junior county sevens' tournament under the leadership of one of the Greig family.

Sevens rugby seems to have increased in popularity at county level during the 1930s with strong Sunderland sides sent to the annual Northumberland tournament. Here they came across representatives from other significant north east teams - Tynedale, Northern, Westoe and Durham City. Tynedale was an old hand at the game - one of its sevens' sides had been the first from England to succeed at the Melrose 7s in the late nineteenth century. Sunderland brought the competition trophy back to Ashbrooke on two occasions; in 1934 and in 1937. Leading light on the sevens' front were club and county players Alan Spence and Geoffrey Cox. As is often the case, two of the leading scorers in the competition did not feature among the most successful at the fifteen-a-side game - in this case T R Jopling and M H Brown.

Reading between the lines, it is possible to see why sevens' rugby failed to gain a really firm foothold. In 1935, the club's decision to enter the Gala Sevens ended in disaster. Sevens' competitions tended to be held towards the end of the season and at Easter in particular. They often clashed with other competitions and with family holidays. The side cobbled together for the competition in the Scottish Borders had to call on help from other Durham clubs and when a vehicle broke down en route, the club was left with a handful of players who crashed out in the first round. Back at Ashbrooke, a 2nd XV fixture had to be cancelled when only ten players turned up. According to the minutes, some ninety players, "members and non-members", had been approached in order to fulfil the holiday fixtures.

On another occasion, the club attempted to run a sevens' competition as a form of knockout to decide on representatives from Durham to attend the Northumberland Sevens. Many senior clubs were invited to attend but in the end a number of junior sides were called on to make up the numbers as only Sunderland and Durham City showed any interest. By the 1936/7 season, players were being asked whether they wanted any Easter fixtures at all

The other interesting development was in relation to **schoolboy and youth rugby**. Thanks to the cuttings' books of Donald Greig and a wonderfully thorough handwritten booklet in the Ashbrooke archives, it is possible to see exactly what went on in this important area during the inter-war period. The rugby club was heavily involved at many levels and the success of schoolboy rugby led later to the growth of a spate of junior clubs in the Sunderland area in the 1930s.

At the beginning of the 1921/2 season, Southwick St Columba's Elementary School from north of the river took on a select side from the Durham City Schools. This was the first match played by a side from the school since 1910 and it ended in a draw. The *Echo* rugby correspondent 'First Reserve' wrote that this game "practically marked the introduction of rugby into the elementary schools of the town". Around 800 spectators, mostly schoolboys, had watched the game where the hard tackling of the raw Sunderland lads was matched by the passing skills of the Durham boys. Within a few weeks, about half a dozen Sunderland schools had taken up the game. A return match between the town and the city was arranged and this led to further schools taking an interest.

Initially it was suggested that games should be "instructive but not competitive" but this idea fell by the wayside. Sunderland 1st XV captain, Stanley Dickinson, the son of an Ashbrooke marine engineering manufacturer, put a trophy up for competition. This was to take place in the New Year of 1922 so the first games played were to be friendlies. The results of these were posted in the *Echo* alongside the results of junior clubs and other schools were encouraged to join in. It was said that there were plenty of 'sturdy lads' in the town as well as young schoolmasters who had learned the game at college and were capable of coaching.

Sunderland RFC also joined the venture with vigour. Schoolboys accompanied by their masters were allowed into 'paying' games for free. Schools were granted use of the club ground for games one afternoon a week and playing members of the club turned up to give encouragement and advice. Posts had also been put up in other areas of the town – at Spark or Spark's Farm and on the new Ford Hall Estate.

All the game reports lead to the conclusion that the school sides were at what we would call 'Under 15' level (i.e., the oldest pupils became 15 in the season in which they were playing). There seems to have been no lower age limit; presumably players were included on grounds of physical size and ability. Both the modern RFU and the local Health and Safety Executive would be shocked to discover that the school teams often took on adult sides. The following observation on such a game comes from the local press:

> "The game's primary objective was to give the schoolboys experience, but I doubt the wisdom of playing the boys…against opponents who are so much older and heavier. It served however to show the capabilities of Wilson, the school full back who performed remarkably well. Although he was giving away about two stones in weight to each of his opponents, he never failed in his tackle, even when he was the only obstacle to (the opposition's) progress."

Shades of a future Mr J Wilkinson perhaps!

In similar matches, the influence of the boys' familiarity with the association game was also evident. This report came after a match between the Junior Tech and Sunderland 3rd XV:

> "As they play both codes, the tendency to adopt 'Soccer' tactics is readily understandable but as soon as they grasp the fact that 'handling' pays best in the Rugby game, they will not be slow in adapting themselves."

By Christmas 1921, Bede Collegiate, the boys' grammar school south of the river, had begun to play. The *Echo* correspondent remarked, "the new starters, as was perhaps natural, were rather prone to offside". St. Columba's won the first town cup. The knockout stage attracted considerable local interest and the final was played at Ashbrooke before a senior match against Percy Park. Ironically it was Frank Pickersgill who presented the trophy. Some years earlier, he had led the campaign to move the Ashbrooke club in the direction of association football.

By the 1922/3 season St. Columba's was recognised as the "foremost schoolboy XV in the county". The side had taken on and defeated a representative side from the Hartlepool schools. The game was played before a match between Hartlepool Rovers and Wakefield and in front of 3,000 spectators. St. Columba's had also topped a merit table based on friendlies and published by the *Echo* at the close of the previous season. Many of the schools that took up the game still exist today, mostly as primary schools. These include Diamond Hall, Barnes and Valley Road Schools.

3.14: Extract from schools' booklet

Sunderland & District Schools' League.

	P	W	L	D	F	a	M	%
St. Columba's	19	16	3	0	348	46	32	84·21
Cowan Terrace	18	12	6	0	289	123	24	66·66
Valley Road	10	6	4	0	139	68	12	60·00
Barnes	19	10	8	1	135	159	21	55·26
Chester Road	15	6	8	1	110	130	13	43·33
Monkwearmouth Central	15	4	9	2	84	219	10	33·33
Diamond Hall	12	3	9	0	42	204	6	25·00
Hendon	3	0	3	0	8	45	0	00·00
St. Andrew's	4	0	4	0	9	140	0	00·00

Around the same time, an equally interesting development took place at under 16 and under 17 level. There appears to have been a genuine concern about the gap between schoolboy rugby and adult rugby - a perennial problem in the game. As the town schools' cup got under way, a meeting was held to form a town union to tackle this problem. The county union, the schools' body and representatives of Sunderland RFC and Southwick Rangers were involved. With many Sunderland youngsters going from school to apprenticeships in the shipyards and engineering works, it was suggested that rugby should be made part of the apprenticeship schemes. To this end, a new league was to be set up and new teams formed to play in the following season.

In the 1922/3 season, the new intermediate league got under way with six teams in it. The games were reported in the local press and a merit table published weekly. By the middle of the season the *Echo* was claiming that Sunderland had 'initiated' an idea that was rapidly spreading to the rest of the county.

The handwritten notebook in the Ashbrooke archives tells the rest of the story, Headed up as "Sunderland rugger with a dash of schoolboy rugby beyond", it is a detailed record of all that happened in schools' and intermediates' rugby between 1921 and 1939. The game seems to have reached its height at this level towards the end of the 1920s. Some eight to ten school teams were playing fourteen-plus league games a season and the results were recorded in a merit table. There was also the town knockout trophy.

The intermediate league seems to have been a huge success. Apprentice sides joined it and soon second and third teams sprang up leading to the development of three leagues. At one point around 1930 there were around thirty school and intermediate sides playing rugby within a league system in the town. Only school results were reported in the booklet in the 1930s.

It is difficult to decide how far the rugby club benefited from this venture - rugby certainly did. It is probable too that many youngsters playing in the 1930s lost their best adult playing days to the war. Whatever the case, there is certainly enough of interest here for modern rugby administrators and coaches to ponder and digest.

Conclusion

Taken all in all, this was perhaps one of the least remarkable periods in the club's history. Despite the developments in schoolboy and intermediate rugby and a spurt of sevens' involvement, little real progress was made. The First World War may have had a great deal to answer for but the signs were already there at the end of the Edwardian period. Early in the 1922/3 season a member of the Scottish Watsonians' club with earlier Sunderland links was so shocked by what he saw at Ashbrooke on a visit that he wrote to the *Echo*. His lengthy observations are worth repeating in full:

"The standard of Rugby football, as evidenced by recent displays at Ashbrooke, can scarcely be regarded as creditable to the town, and it seems incomprehensible that Sunderland, which holds a good position in other sports, should be unable to field a Rugger XV, competent to put up a respectable fight against the teams of neighbouring towns whose population is smaller, and whose players have no greater opportunities of learning the art of Rugby. This state of affairs is the more regrettable when one learns that serious efforts are being made this season by the authorities responsible to improve the status of the game locally, and it is with some diffidence therefore that an onlooker ventures to make some suggestions that are put forward in no destructive spirit.

"It is evident that no players of outstanding ability are available for the team; on the other hand, there exists considerable keenness among many of the players. This is the position in which two of the Edinburgh sides found themselves at periods during the last fifteen years. The Watsonians, about 1907-8, had few or no really good men. Play was incoherent and opportunistic and defeats were more frequent than palatable. The Committee was faced with training difficulties owing to members being engaged in business up to an hour which precluded training in the evening, and by the fact that distances between players' houses and the field were considerably greater than in Sunderland, but these obstacles were overcome by the keen players. Training was performed before breakfast on three or four fixed mornings a week, halves and three quarters training apart from the forwards.

"The forwards practised dribbling, special attention being directed to ball control, then to packing and wheeling, and finally to passing by hand, a feature one rarely sees among forwards in this part of the world.

"The backs trained first of all without the ball in order to learn their positions, next practised quick long passes and later co-ordination of different forms of attack between halves and threes.

"It soon became obvious that turning out to these practices was essential to a place on the team; if a man did not turn up, he was dropped and the possibly slightly inferior player from the second team got his place, the relative mediocrity of these players making this somewhat severe step less risky than might at first appear. The results were gradual but definite. The team consolidated and, although defeats continued throughout the season, the games were better and more enjoyable. The system was applied in the following season, and the team finished up Scottish champions without losing a match, and with three or four internationals in the side.

"A season or two before the war, the scheme was adopted by another Edinburgh team, Heriotonians, who also finished up by winning the championship. There seems to be no reason why it should not be adopted in Sunderland.

"I would only add, 'Now, Sunderland players, what are you going to do about it?'"

'Nuff said! And if the tone appears a little too serious, a lighter note to end upon, as it is worth reflecting on how much some of the *Echo* reporters knew about the game of rugby (or 'rubgy' as it was once headlined). On another occasion, the newspaper had Sunderland 1st XV playing the first half of the game against Percy Main (a Tyneside cricket team) and the second half against Percy Park (the real opponents). Familiarity with the association game also reared its head as when, due to a single injured player, "Sunderland XV was reduced to ten men". In fairness to the *Echo,* its coverage of rugby was usually very thorough and the local newspaper had been a considerable help when it came to spreading the game's popularity.

If Sunderland RFC was to return to its glory days, it would have to take heed of the criticisms levelled at it by is former supporter. The future seemed to lie in teamwork, training and coaching as well as personal fitness and self-discipline. Perhaps these would develop in the years following the second great conflict.

Chapter Four
From War to Celebration (1945-1974)

The post-war period chosen stretches from the end of the Second World War to the celebration of a hundred years of club rugby in Sunderland during the 1973/4 season. It was a time that saw a number of club members playing key roles in the development of rugby at club, county and national level, and in some cases beyond. The most prominent of these were Eric Watt Moses, Alan Bean, Hartley Elliott and Robin Auld and their stories are told elsewhere (see Appendix Two). For Sunderland RFC, the period was mainly about finding suitable fixtures, developing youngsters, introducing coaching and, inevitably, finding ways of paying for it all.

Post-war Problems

As early as September 1944, key officials of the club got together to discuss the future. Eric Watt Moses, Alan Bean, Donald Greig and Major Kayll (father of rugby-playing air ace Joe, who was a prisoner of war at the time) were all present. They agreed to anticipate the restart of rugby by targeting youngsters who had continued to play the game at public schools. When hostilities came to an end in 1945, the committee allowed the use of Ashbrooke for public school trials and offered all players free membership until the end of the year.

The war continued to cause problems for ten years or more after it had ended. Repairing the damage caused by air raids and recovering the resultant costs took a long time and the archives are packed with correspondence between the club and various official bodies, stretching well into the 1950s. Rationing lasted for an equally long time, causing headaches with regards to kit and playing equipment. Players and supporters saved up special coupons in order to buy new shirts and shorts, and for a long period such purchases were undertaken by the club rather than by individuals. At one point a special effort was put in to find coupons in order to buy one spare pair of shorts for each of the teams.

As in the First World War, lives had been lost and playing careers considerably shortened. In the programme for the 1946 international trial held at Ashbrooke, one writer noted that the clubs in Durham County alone had lost 133 rugby players, including eight who had earned county caps. Sunderland RFC's losses are recorded in the previous chapter. The ever-alert Eric Watt Moses, then county secretary, was moved to set up a County Players' Memorial Fund. The idea was to raise £1,000 and to make the money available to clubs, as loans with low rates of interest. The money could be spent on ground improvement and equipment. Sunderland RFC responded swiftly and raised 10% of the desired total by organising a bowls match, a cricket match and a raffle. The £1,000 target was passed in a very short time although the Sunderland club agreed to make no immediate call on the money. The fund continued to be topped up and used to support schoolboy rugby in the county for many years after the conflict.

Neither was administrative life easy shortly after 1945. The government introduced a complex entertainment tax, which had to be paid on various types of sporting income and involved detailed record-keeping. Despite complaints at every level (including the committee at Sunderland RFC) the law was not scrapped until 1953. Towards the end of the period, VAT also began to rear its ugly head.

The Game Continues

The 1st XV was in action soon after the war in the Far East came to an end and played its first match in late September 1945. The 2nd XV fixtures began in December of the same year, but the 3rd XV had to wait until the beginning of the following season. With the 1950s came a 4th XV, and by 1960 a 5th XV which consisted mainly of youngsters. Not wishing to be stigmatised as 'fifth' best the players asked for the team to be renamed. Thus Ashbrooke Rovers was born. By the early 1960s, the club was able to put out six teams including two teams of colts.

Fixtures

Clearly the club was booming in terms of playing members and the authors of *To Ashbrooke and Beyond* described the immediate post-war years as years 'filled with vitality' on the field of play. However this was a time when a rugby club was judged by quality rather than quantity, and club organisers regarded the strength of the fixture list as a key benchmark. Up to the introduction of leagues in the 1980s, the fixtures' secretary was one of the most important men on the club committee, and had to get it right. Neither success against weak sides nor failure against strong sides was deemed acceptable; the most desirable situation was one where a string of consistently good results led to an improved fixture list a few seasons later.

From the late 1940s to the early 1970s, Sunderland RFC seems to have regarded itself as a club just tucked in behind the 'big boys' of the region. When a league for top clubs in the area was proposed in the 1960s, the club committee opposed the idea. Not only were members against the league, they also felt that, were it to be formed, the club's 1st XV would not be invited to join it.

Sunderland's position in the pecking order is reflected in its fixture lists; the club continued to play against all the old rivals from the region as well as a number of rising junior clubs. Games away to Richmond and home to a travelling Ebbw Vale were approached with considerable excitement. A number of sides from Yorkshire and Cumberland became regular opponents as well as teams from north of the border. The season's opener was often against Yorkshire's Old Leodensians and there was a special relationship with Cumberland's Keswick. Other regulars included Ilkley, Otley, Harrogate, Bradford, Wigton and Egremont. Heaton Moor and Moortown were also old friends, as was Jedforest.

The playing season also had a recognisable structure. Annual fixtures with Durham City took place over the Christmas/New Year holiday and the club made arrangements to have special fixtures around the time of the Calcutta Cup between England and Scotland. When the international was in Scotland, an Edinburgh University side provided the opposition with Beckenham an opponent when the international took place at Twickenham. Easter tours were also popular and usually successful. Visits to West Cumberland, North Yorkshire and Lancashire all took place during this period and a trip to Sweden in the early 1950s was described as "missionary". Occasionally touring sides dropped in too.

Towards the end of the post-war period, the club also set up an early season fixture with the Dolphins XV. This was an ad-hoc side founded by former Sunderland player and international referee Hartley Elliott and playing under his name until the middle of the 1960s. It often contained a number of Scottish internationals. Fixtures took place between Sunderland's 1st XV and the Dolphins in 1971 and 1972 as well as during the 1973/4 centenary season. There was also a Dolphins fixture with America's Princeton University at Ashbrooke in March 1972. Between its foundation and 1973, the Dolphins boasted 12 British Lions and 86 international players in its side. In the centenary programme it was noted that the aim of the Dolphins was to play "exhibition rugby with that spirit of enjoyment that does not always attend the modern game".

Sunderland Cricket & Rugby Football Club

Rugby   Section

1873   1973

Centenary   Programme

SUNDERLAND

V

The DOLPHINS

Ashbrooke
K.O. 6.30 p.m.
Wednesday, September 5th 1973

Price 15p

4.1: Programme of match against Dolphins, 1973

The Games

The 1945 to 1974 period is not an easy one to analyse in terms of success and failure. In the final analysis, inconsistency seems to have been the key word for most of the club's sides. Cup success for both the 1st and 2nd XV in 1959 (see below) came in the middle of a mini golden patch, which lasted into the early 1960s. Victories over Hartlepool Rovers, West Hartlepool, Tynedale, Durham and Blaydon were recorded during this period with the 1958/9 season regarded as "the most pleasing for many years". During the 1960/61 season only 34 out of the 134 games played by the club sides were lost, and talk was of excellent fitness, spirit and morale throughout. The 1968/9 season during which the 1st XV won 20 out of 30 games was described as the "most successful" for years. The club also gathered on-field momentum towards the centenary season of 1973/4. Things appear to have been at their best when players "played hard and enjoyed the comradeship to the full".

Set against this is season after season when sides throughout the club recorded a negative outcome, winning less than 50% of their fixtures. More than one season was written of as "one to forget" at the reflective AGM. A poor 1956/7 set of results was put down to lack of confidence among players, and the early 1950s in general were disappointing although this may have been the consequence of an over-ambitious fixture list as attempts were made to produce a 1st XV "comparable to the best North East and Yorkshire Clubs". When things were at their worst, few turned up for training. A 'no train, no play' policy was adopted and rapidly abandoned when it became difficult to fulfil fixtures. The success of the early 1960s seems to have come to an end with the loss of a complete front row through retirement, removal and university demands. The 1964/5 season was described as "mediocre" with 2nds and 3rds standing their ground, while the 1st XV won only a third of its games. The 1966/7 season was one of "unfulfilled promise", likewise at the end of 1972, when it was noted that improvement was needed if the club was to stay anywhere near the local 'top flight'.

In the middle of this inconsistency are hidden massive efforts on the part of club officials to improve things and, and as noted more than once in the minutes, to "gain better fixtures". After a stint as President of the RFU (see Appendix Two), Eric Watt Moses returned to the club, determined to put into operation practice he had observed in the Southern Hemisphere. He was in the rugby club chair from 1950-1953 and, under his guidance, big changes were made. The committee started to meet in early summer to elect the captains, and the first eight weeks of training contained a twenty-minute session with a PT instructor. Six current and former players acted as coaches, dealing in what we would now call 'unit skills', whilst details of training attendances were kept in a book and affected selection decisions. Top players (like a wartime English hooker) gave talks on positional play and films of the New Zealanders in action were shown. A library was set up in the club and loop films borrowed to be shown on a 16mm projector. This meant that a positional skill could be observed over and over again. A librarian volunteered to look after relevant books and films.

Out on the field, the scrummaging machine was re-upholstered, skipping ropes were purchased to be used indoors in wet weather and players were told that most practice nights would be dedicated to teamwork; they were now responsible for individual skills. Lighting arrangements were also updated in order to improve the quality of training.

In the late 1950s, a poor season's end led to the setting-up of a summer school. Initially it was for senior players with the aim of improving individual skills and fitness but gradually youngsters were invited to join in. This event eventually turned into an under 20s' and schoolboys' school to stop it declining into sessions described in the minutes as "old boys playing touch". Some on the committee also felt that the older players needed a summer break in order to restore health and fitness.

Many of the most interesting developments came in the 1960s when club man Robin Auld was heavily involved in raising the profile of coaching at county and national level (See Appendix Two). At one meeting of the club committee, Robin flagged up the need to coach players to "read the game" and to play as a team. In 1969, there were lengthy discussions about appointing a club coach. Ex-England and British Lion Mike Weston was approached but he had already committed himself to Durham City. Eventually the committee appointed former player and knowledgeable referee Ken Witherington to the position. Over the next few years - with input from the likes of Harry Wilson, Larry Dowell, Ian Hind and Frank Greenshields - coaching became a regular part of the club setup. A number of these attended coaching courses held in the county and at the RFU centre at Lilleshall.

4.2: Ken Witherington at an Ashbrooke coaching course (centre
- blonde hair and dark kit)

In analysing the rugby club's success and failure during the 1945-74 period, events on the field of play do not lend themselves easily to firm conclusions. The magnificent efforts to improve made in the early 1950s seem to have had no immediate effect on results (although it could be argued that they laid the foundations for success in the late 1950s and 1960s). The same could be said too of the efforts of the late 1960s - although it is possible that they came to fruition in the centenary year. What becomes increasingly clear from all the records is that success was down to players out on the field. If they were prepared to work at their fitness as individuals, to develop their individual skills, to attend training and to work at team tactics then all went well. In this respect, the 1920s critic had it right (see end of the previous chapter). What drives a group of players to act in this manner may remain a mystery - and one that the organisers of many an amateur rugby club would love to solve. Alternatively it could be argued that the change often takes time to work its way through and to have a positive effect.

1973-4: A Special Season

In the late 1960s, the club committee realised that it was close to the club's centenary and chose the 1973/4 season for celebratory events. Research carried out both before and after the centenary shows this to have been an appropriate choice. With Robin Auld in the chair and the support of players past and present, the season proved to be a memorable one. Robin kept a thorough record of proceedings and has been kind enough to place the resultant file in the archives.

SUNDERLAND R.F.C.

FIXTURE LIST 1973 — 74

5 Sept.	The Dolphins XV	home	1 Jan.	Durham City	away
8 Sept.	Ryton	home	3 Jan.	Northern	home
15 Sept.	Leodiensians	away	12 Jan.	Percy Park	away
22 Sept.	Ilkley	home	19 Jan.	North Durham	home
29 Sept.	Durham County Presidents XV	home	26 Jan.	Middlesbrough	away
6 Oct.			2 Feb.	Workington	away
13 Oct.	Morpeth	away	9 Feb.	Novos	away
20 Oct.	Darlington	away	16 Feb.	Egremont	home
27 Oct.	Newcastle Univ.	home	23 Feb.	Durham Univ.	home
3 Nov.	Stockton	away			
10 Nov.	Wigton	home	2 March	Mowden Park	away
17 Nov.	Gosforth	away	9 March	Blaydon	away
24 Nov.	Westoe	home	16 March	Scarborough	home
			23 March	Tynedale	home
1 Dec.	Cup		30 March	Jedforest	home
8 Dec.	Carlisle	home	3 April	Hartlepool Rovers	home
15 Dec.	Gateshead Fell	away	6 April	Redcar	home
22 Dec.	Alnwick	away	13 April	Hull and E.R.	home
26 Dec.	Durham City	home	14 April	West Hartlepool	home
29 Dec.			20 April		

4.3: Fixture list for the centenary season

The fixture list for the 1973/4 season was bound to be a little special. It included the traditional Boxing Day game with Durham City and a match with Scottish

Borders' side, Jedforest. There was also a September curtain-raiser against the Dolphins and a match with a County President's XV later in the same month. In addition, the centenary committee organised a reunion match for players and a centenary dinner. The latter was held at the Top Rank Suite in October 1973 with the President of the RFU Micky Steele Bodger as guest speaker. Robin Auld's archive of photographs shows it to have been a successful affair. The 1973 centenary committee reads like a 'Who's Who?' of Sunderland rugby. It included David Boyd, Alan Towers, Hughie Lamb, Eric Watt Moses, Alan Bean, Hartley Elliott, Adam Scott Gray and Robin Auld.

The two September games brought a number of well-known players to Ashbrooke. Even with late cry-offs, the Dolphins' side was an experienced one. It included Hannaford of Bristol, Robinson of Gosforth and Cowell of Rugby, all England internationals. Hannah and Turk, playing in the backs, were both Scottish internationals. The President's XV included Scottish international and British Lion Alan Tomes. The committee set up to organise celebrations decided that the seasonal extras should be self-funding and to that end sought donations from former players. It also raised £400 from a sponsored run.

For the 1st XV, the 1973/4 season was a very good playing season, in fact one of the best in the club's history, and was thus described in the AGM minutes. Significant victories, including a big one over Hartlepool Rovers, were offset by annoyingly close losses to other major sides. Overall it is a season remembered for a balance of youth and experience in the side - a side that was well coached by the evergreen Harry Wilson. The 1st XV lost a mere seven out of its 34 games and scored 816 points against 316 while the 2nd XV won two-thirds of its games.

The Players

As noted earlier in this chapter, there were times during this period when almost a hundred senior and colt players were turning out for the club on Saturdays. This makes a section on players a most difficult one to put together. Indeed, the committee was keen to stress the importance of teamwork and the Players' Trophy, first awarded to long-serving Charles Ranken in 1960, eventually became a team award.

On a wider playing front there were a couple of important developments in this period. In the first instance, the collapse of junior club Old Bedans in the middle of the 1960s brought an influx of new players into the Sunderland club. The Bede Grammar School, on the same side of the river as Ashbrooke, had been supported by the Sunderland SRFC as it developed the game, as had the junior rugby club which was set up primarily for former pupils. Members of the school staff were also among players and officials at the Ashbrooke club.

An equally interesting development came with the movement of a number of players to Ashbrooke from other junior clubs. Many of them had learned the game as schoolboys and apprentices in the leagues set up before the Second World War. This led to a broadening of the social structure of the club's players although, with a number of exceptions, many had still attended rugby-playing public schools or grammar schools.

As in previous chapters, the roles of many of the prominent players will be discussed in the representative and county sections. Other players worthy of a mention include the ageless John Hedley who was a 1st XV regular from the 1950s onwards and played in the 1959 cup-winning side. He later became a respected referee, and can still be seen in and around the club when he visits as a referee assessor, more than half a century later. Adam Scott Gray falls into the same category and it is difficult to sum up adequately his contribution to the rugby club both on and off the field. He took charge of a number of successful XVs in the 1950s before switching to administration and his work with fixtures and as secretary is deserving of the highest praise. The minutes he produced were full, detailed and a joy to read and, without them, this book would not have been possible.

Charles W Pickersgill, yet another in an Ashbrooke family line, played and captained one of the sides in the early 1950s. Max Deas, later to become a local television personality, was a keen rugby player, an all-round sportsman and tireless administrator. He was also responsible for Ashbrooke's huge and priceless collection of rugby club shields; there were over two hundred of these by the late 1970s. From Valley Road Old Boys came the immortal Jimmy Lee. Jimmy was renowned for his toughness on the field and was immensely popular. He and his wife became the wider club's first stewards in 1950s. He later took over as groundsman and continued to serve the club into the 1980s. Bill Brown, ex-St Gabriel's, was another who came through the school and local junior club system. Neville Boyd, brother of county player David, was also a popular member of the club. According to the minutes, his marriage was responsible for the cancellation of all the club's fixtures on one particular Saturday; in later life he moved to the Northumberland coast. Bill Stuart was captain for five seasons including 1959 when the 1st XV last won the senior County Cup. When he moved away from Sunderland in the 1970s, he had been a club member for thirty years and a valuable administrator. Dale, McKinley, Bell, Fairley, Bellerby, Collings, Wood, Harrison and Hardy were other surnames often featured on team sheets and in the club minutes.

4.4: A representative selection of Ashbrooke shields

As time progressed, new talent began to emerge. Derek Blair, who played his county rugby for Northumberland, came into the side and captained it in the late 1960s. Like Larry Dowell, another tough-tackling forward, he was later to become involved in coaching. Harry Wilson, still a club regular in 2011 and young star of the show in 1959, captained the side in 1970 and also took a great interest in coaching. Ian Hind, later highly influential in the development of mini rugby, moved up from schoolboy rugby to captain the 1st XV. By the time of the centenary, the influential Bentley brothers - Charlie and Colin - were on the scene. Future junior school Headmaster and junior coach Peter McCarron featured in the forwards, as a host of colts began to make their way into senior sides. Pillars of the club such as future referee Steve Thompson, Paul Sturgess and Charlie Dixon were starting to appear on team sheets. Charlie Dixon, the Nicholson brothers (John and Peter) and Cumbrian Graham Young were also elemental to the success of the 1st XV around the time of the centenary. Peter Nicholson went on to take charge of the club's junior rugby in the 1990s. Dave

Hodgson, future 1st XV captain and club coach, also appeared on the scene around this time.

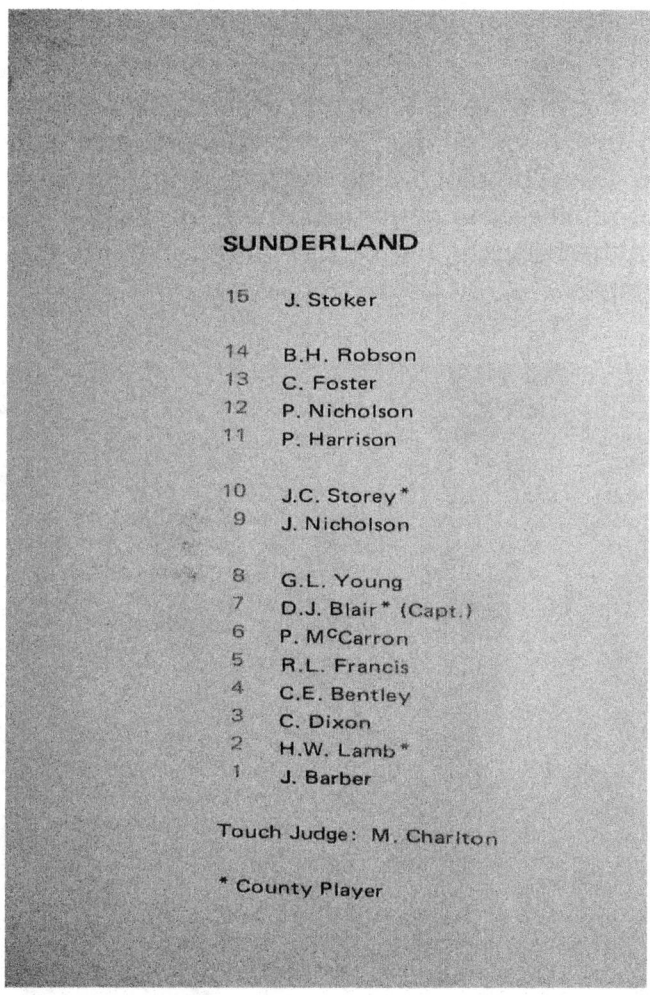

SUNDERLAND

15   J. Stoker

14   B.H. Robson
13   C. Foster
12   P. Nicholson
11   P. Harrison

10   J.C. Storey*
9   J. Nicholson

8   G.L. Young
7   D.J. Blair* (Capt.)
6   P. McCarron
5   R.L. Francis
4   C.E. Bentley
3   C. Dixon
2   H.W. Lamb*
1   J. Barber

Touch Judge: M. Charlton

* County Player

4.5: *1st XV team sheet from the centenary season*

While on the subject of players, it is interesting to note the increasing appearance in the minutes of references to behaviour on and off the pitch. This was a time when disciplinary committees began to appear and every now and then players were hauled up before them and reprimanded or suspended. In the early 1970s, a letter was received from a local hotel complaining about the damage caused during a club dinner. (In defence of players from this period, in

1934, the committee had to pay 11/6 [58p] in damages to the Palatine Hotel after a similar debacle!)

More interesting perhaps is the emergence of post-match rowdiness on the bus and in the bar. The minutes contain frequent and amusing references to singing, presumably of what came to be known as 'rugby songs'. Eventually the committee decreed that such singing could take place directly after the match but away from the ears of discerning people enjoying a drink in the bars. Significantly one committee member described the songs themselves as "not too bad". Singing on the bus was banned for a period in the early 1970s; time for a brief chuckle perhaps.

4.6: Ahead of their time - players from the 1950s apply dance techniques to training

County Cups

For most of this period, the annual Durham Senior Cup continued to be a prestigious affair and success in the competition was still regarded as an important measure of a club's standing. Sunderland RFC enjoyed very little in the way of success in this area with the 1st XV making only three finals between the late 1940s, (when the competition restarted), and 1974. Twice they ended on the losing side, going down to Hartlepool Rovers 14-0 in 1948 and to Westoe 6-0 in 1950.

The single 1st XV cup success came in 1959. It was the first one since 1931 and the last one to date - so rare, in fact that a 50th annual reunion was held in 2009. In the final, the club defeated old rivals Durham City 6-3. Club stalwart Harry Wilson, only a teenager at the time, played in the match and has vivid memories of post-match celebrations. So good were they that he forgot to bring his boots for the official team photograph and was thus positioned on the back row of the picture so that his feet were not in view. This cup success has lessons for the game in general as it was achieved by a team which balanced youth and experience. In it were David Boyd, Hughie Lamb, the long-serving Charles Ranken, future referees John Hedley and Ken Witherington plus, Bill Stuart and Alan Towers.

4.7: Durham Senior Challenge Cup winning side, 1959

The 1958/9 season was made all the sweeter by similar success in the 2nd XV trophy. The Seconds were victorious over Westoe 8-6; only 23 points were scored in two finals - a rare occurrence in the modern game. J A Wood, captain of the 2nd XV, had the honour of playing in both finals thanks to a last minute injury to a 1st XV player.

The 2nd XV was quite strong in the mid-to-late1950s, making two other finals. It defeated Hartlepoool Rovers 9-6 in the 1956 final and lost to Blaydon 9-6 in the following year. The 3rd XV had a single cup success during the period, defeating Hartlepool Rovers 11-6 in 1961, while the 4th XV lost to Westoe in the final of the same year. The 2nd XV also lost the 1965 final 6-0 to Gateshead Fell, with the 3rds going down to Durham County in 1966. In 1969 the 2nds, 3rds and 4ths all made finals - and lost!

Details of the Senior Cup between the late 1940s and early 1970s reflect on the strengths of certain clubs. Hartlepool Rovers and Durham City were dominant here with occasional forays from West Hartlepool and Blaydon. At the same time there were signs that the cup system was becoming less attractive and, in some cases, a nuisance to those who enjoyed a prestigious fixture programme. On one occasion in the 1950s, Hartlepool Rovers asked to withdraw from the 1st XV trophy for this reason. On another, Billingham suggested that the cup be scrapped altogether. The Sunderland committee still saw the various trophies as an essential boost to team spirit.

Throughout this period, the Ashbrooke pitch was still in demand for various County Cup finals at senior and junior level. In 1972, however, a request to hold the senior final there had to be turned down due to resurfacing of the pitch.

Sevens

Throughout the 1945-1974 period, the shorter version of the game was a secondary interest. The only sevens' tournament entered on a regular basis was the Durham County one, held at Billingham towards the end of the season. Here Sunderland's entries were sporadic and, on one occasion, the club was informed that it was the only senior one in the county not sending a side. The reasons for this lack of commitment are clear. Early season competitions such as those held at Northumberland club Northern carried risk of injury to those just setting up for the longer game. The increasingly popular Easter 7s caused problems when it came to raising sides due to holiday arrangements and club tours. To the club's embarrassment, it had to withdraw twice from the Wigton 7s, after agreeing to participate.

Among the sevens offered and rejected were those held at Bridlington and Workington. In the early 1960s, flushed by County Cup victory, the club entered the Esher sevens, and in the mid 60s won the county event. Otherwise there was little in the way of sevens' joy.

Coaching the Youngsters

As in the years immediately after the First World War, the club took a great interest in youth rugby after the second global conflict. With a packed fixture list, concern for the future and improvement in the club's standing led to a drive to attract the most promising youngsters in the area whatever their social background.

The development of youth rugby in this period is often difficult to follow due to the terminology used. Generally, schools' rugby took place at under 15 level, although at the grammar and public schools, the main school sides were drawn from those aged 16 to 18 years - in the 6th form. There seems to have been a tendency to call all in this category "schoolboys". Thus at times, club under 18 sides were only allowed to play four "schoolboys" and the rest had not to be in full time education. A successful Sunderland club side of the 1970s was said to be a "genuine" colts' side without any "schoolboys".

The Sunderland club began to look at schools' rugby closely in the early 1950s, mainly as a result of a county directive. The target seems to have been under 15s at the non-rugby playing schools. Visits to such schools showed that the majority of Headteachers favoured soccer, and also that few staff members had experienced rugby at school or college. A meeting was set up with the Chief Education Officer and members of the county rugby committee, but little progress seems to have been made. When a talented schoolboy was spotted, he was invited to train with the seniors. One of these was a young Jackie Washington who, sadly for the sport of rugby, later turned his attention to cricket, football and bowls. One tale tells of how he kept goal in the FA Amateur Cup Final wearing his Sunderland Cricket Club cap.

An eye was also kept on schools where rugby was played and throughout this period the club organised fixtures for them during the Christmas holidays. The opposition was drawn from other rugby clubs scattered around the north east.

The club's summer school, initially intended for seniors, gradually moved to being totally dedicated to juniors. A local boy, Michael Miller, was chosen to represent England Schools and, towards the end of the period, dossiers were kept on the most promising schoolboys. The committee supported efforts to create bonds with schools and youth organisations including the Bede Grammar School, north of the river, and Monkwearmouth Grammar School to the south. It also made contact with Red House School and Lambton Street Boys' Club while Tonstall School, a local private school, made frequent use of Ashbrooke facilities.

As noted earlier, it is often difficult to work out exactly what was going on with younger players at club level. Immediately after the war, Durham County staged what it claimed to be the first age-limit colts' match in the country - one in which the county defeated Cumberland and Westmorland by 17 points to 3. By the 1950s, a Sunderland Cup for under 18s was in place; ironically the Sunderland club was not able to raise a side. By the middle of the 1950s, the club had a side in place and the under 18s made two finals in 1955 and 1957. Both were lost but it is gratifying to note that some of the players in those teams were to serve the club well at a future date. At the same time many at this age group were regularly taking the field for senior 4th and 5th XVs. In some cases there seemed to have been an unwritten understanding that games involving these sides were age limited. At one point, club committee members were distressed to find that the 4th XV had come up against "an opposition packed with seasoned players". It was suggested that enquiries be made in the future about the ages of the opposition.

Colts' rugby, as we know it today, appears to have taken off seriously at the club in the middle of the 1960s. A really strong side was developed and for a couple of idyllic seasons, it rarely lost a game. The lynchpin here was local boy Eric Walton who quickly rose to county level, and to captaincy of the county colts. Paul Jobling, Dave Hodgson, Eric Blakey and John Tate soon joined him. Paul Jobling came close to national recognition and the others were all to give stout service to the senior club both as players and coaches. In 1969 another colt, Steve Harrison, offered to run the line for the 1st XV and thus started years of club involvement which eventually saw all three sons playing at senior level. Eddie Collins - heavily involved in junior coaching and administration still - started his long and successful playing career in the colts and received one of the first annual player awards. By 1972, the colts were in safe hands and being coached by future senior county captain and coach Charlie Bentley.

There were a couple of interesting downsides to colts' rugby. Those involved regularly played two games on a Saturday - for the school in the morning and the colts in the afternoon. Many schools objected and in the early 1970s, Durham County committee made a "non-binding" objection to the practice. Club members also became frustrated as year in, year out, senior sides failed to benefit from colt progress as the lads moved away to college and university - a common complaint among English rugby clubs.

In the 50s, 60s and 70s, as today, the retention of 15-18 year olds in the game of rugby was a priority. During the period in question there were constant discussions over the way in which the club could alleviate the cost of membership to these players and also provide them with some form of acceptable social life. The outcome makes for interesting reading (see Appendix One).

There are also many around the club today who started their careers under this regime. Steve Harrison tells of how he had his nose badly battered in a school match one Saturday morning and was advised by his coach (also an Ashbrooke man) not to play for the club colts in the afternoon. Steve ignored the advice and went to the club, where he was promptly put into the 4th XV, which was a man short. Those who have played 4th XV rugby will appreciate that the condition of Steve's nose deteriorated considerably in the ensuing conflict!

The Committee

By the 1950s there had been considerable changes in the make-up of the rugby club committee since the early days at Chester Road. By now, the Byelaws stated clearly that no player could be a committee member unless under exceptional circumstances and then only on an ex-officio basis. Captains were invited to attend meetings and the minutes for 1953 reveal that 1st XV captain Bill Stuart was phoned at home and told that he had been re-elected and could now make his way to the meeting. This was a far cry from Victorian era when the players and the committee were one and the same.

The committee had also grown in numbers due to co-options. At one point in this period there were over 20 names on the list although, at times, attendance at meetings ran only to 50%. In the early 70s, a minute was recorded making the weekly meeting for selection and urgent matters, with only one meeting per month a business meeting. In practice, the minutes show there to have been little real change.

One of the main aims of the committee was to keep the club on a sound financial basis and this frequently involved discussion with the wider sports club (see Appendix One). Self-sufficiency was seen as the magic end, if a difficult one to achieve. Income came from gate money from time to time (although it is not clear whether some, or all, of this went directly to the wider club). A cup semi final against Blaydon not too long after the war charged entry of 1/6 for adults and 6d for boys. County games in the 60s cost 2/- for the ground, and an extra 1/- to sit in the stand. A University Cup final held at Ashbrooke cost 4/- to watch and, under decimalisation in the early 1970s it was 10p to enter the stand.

Match fees were taken from the players (who also had to be members of the wider club). Fees started at about 1/- (5p) a game after the Second World War and were increased on a regular basis with the 1st XV often expected to pay more than other sides. Towards the end of the period they were up to 3/6 (18p) a game. Another source of income came from selling match programmes from time to time - a source which proved most profitable when costs were covered by advertising so that sales were recorded as pure profit.

In truth, the fees and entrance/programme money raised relatively little, and the main source of revenue came from the efforts of a select group of individuals who formed the entertainments committee. Over the 1945-1974 period, this committee embarked upon numerous fundraising ventures - football sweeps and draws, horse racing sweeps, bingo, club nights, men-only nights, dinner dances, discos, fireworks, Christmas draws, Easter draws etc.; the income generated was invaluable. The fireworks display drew thousands to Ashbrooke and by 1973 was clearing over £300 in profit. On one occasion, a member's illness meant that no arrangements had been made for the Easter draw, so another committee member went out immediately and purchased a top of the range watch, wound it up and accepted payment for guesses as to when it would stop. The prize was the watch, and the hastily organised (and possibly illegal) competition raised the amount required.

As a rule, the entertainments committee raised close to £300 a season and, on one occasion, handed over £500 - a considerable amount in the 1950s, and over half the cost of running the rugby club. A weekly draw club in the 1960s was particularly successful but was soon taken over by the wider club. Skilled fundraisers received frequent praise in the minutes including the evergreen Jimmy Lee, Charles W Pickersgill and the redoubtable 'Chappie' Harrison. In the 1950s, Chappie was getting rugby players and supporters to put their hands in their pockets; in 2011, he was still doing the same to the bowls players. "Without this we just could not carry on," a club committee member noted at one point.

The awkward question of player insurance was raised on a number of occasions. After consultation with the RFU, it was decided that the club could not afford a global policy and individuals should make their own arrangements. This did not really solve the problem and there were a few cases of genuine hardship when players with broken legs actually lost wages. The club had devised an emergency fund - at one point buying a set of the new premium bonds as collateral and then buying more after a big win on the earlier bonds! In the middle of the 1960s the 'Injury Fund' stood at £130 and on at least two occasions injured players were helped out by the fund, and also by other cash raised from collections from players in the senior sides. Committee members also visited players in hospital on a regular basis.

Other interesting titbits can also be picked up from club minutes. In February 1953, the RFU asked the committee for its opinions on televising international rugby. After debate, it was agreed to support the transmission of two games per season from Twickenham and one each from Murrayfield and Cardiff. A minute from the 1951/2 season also gives us chapter and verse on the club's striping - four inches of red, three inches of yellow and two inches of black. This makes the strip recognisably different from that of sides using the same striping. In the days when the north east of England is providing the captain of a successful England Ladies' side, it also seems strange to find the ladies attached to the rugby section making tea and fundraising. Whatever the case, their contribution was invaluable, and appreciation of their help and support gained numerous references at committee meetings.

Other issues that took up as much committee time as the search for a second ground included the provision of floodlighting for training purposes and decent bathing facilities. In the early 1960s, £300 was borrowed to install improved lighting.

Many administrators made significant contributions during the post-war period but Joe Fairley and former cup-winning captain Roy Wilson deserve special mentions. Both served the club well over a long period of time.

Pitches

A major issue throughout this period and indeed throughout the history of the club has been that of the pitch. For years, the club survived on having the single pitch at Ashbrooke as its only playing surface, with either 1st XV or 2nd XV playing there while other teams were fulfilling away fixtures. The pitch itself was creating problems by the post-war period. Built over old mine workings and based on poor foundations, it has always "acted up". At one point in this period a violent storm brought broken glass and stone to the surface and caused a game to be cancelled. In the 1960s the flooding was so bad that action had to be taken and a new drainage system put in.

4.8: Ashbrooke at midsummer; rugby stand and pitch and cricket pitches visible (former hockey pitch at bottom)

As the number of teams being put out by the club each Saturday grew, so too did the pitch issue. Soon after the war, the committee asked the local council if a pitch could be established in nearby Backhouse Park. The request was turned down, even though the club sent a high powered delegation to argue the case. As schoolboy rugby came into the picture in the early 1950s, the matter was broached again. It was then discovered that the council had another of the club's favoured spots put aside for building.

By the mid-1950s, the club had established good relationships with TLF Sports or 'Belford House' - an RFU affiliated junior club half a mile to the south and there was some talk of pitch sharing. At first, the new club put out a single side consisting mainly of local teenagers and shared their pitch with the Sunderland club, in return for a set of posts and training advice. By 1956, Belford House was looking to put out its own 2nd XV and warned the established club that it would have to look elsewhere. In the same year, Sunderland AFC also came in with an offer which at the time was "difficult to refuse", although, in the end, nothing came of it (see Appendix One).

By the late 1950s, the need for another pitch had turned attentions southwards along the Ryhope Road, to a farmer's field about a mile from Ashbrooke. The Church Commissioners rented the field to a farmer (who had a rugby-playing son). Thanks to the hard work of Brian Mair, the club obtained a short-term lease on the field and began to play 2nd and 3rd XV games there. The ground, however, was not considered suitable for 1st XV rugby and the farmer still seemed to wish to plough it up from time to time! Three years later, this second ground was purchased from the church commissioners through a combination of donations and loans - including one of £3,000 at 2% from the RFU.

'Ryhope Road' remained a club ground until the dying years of the twentieth century. It was not without its problems, as it was situated over a mile from Ashbrooke and difficult to keep secure when games were not being played. Wooden huts as changing rooms were burnt down while talk of a more permanent indoor centre there was seen as moving the heart of the rugby club away from Ashbrooke and breaking age-old ties. As early as the 1970s, some committee members were looking to sell the ground and move on. However, as was noted in the 1960s, Sunderland RFC at least had another ground which covered nine acres, and where they could "play three games in a day".

County Level and Special

During the post-war period, Durham County enjoyed another purple patch. A county history, written in the 1970s, claimed that its achievements here matched those of the county in Edwardian times and, though this claim does not really hold up to scrutiny, it is not without some foundation. Only one major national success was achieved yet it could be argued that county rugby in general had strengthened over the years and the opposition to be overcome was far stronger than in years past. As in former days, players from Sunderland RFC had a significant role to play in what success there was.

By the 1950s, the structure of the County Championship had changed. Success in the Northern group now led to a semi final rather than a final. Between 1958 and 1968, Durham County topped the northern group on six occasions and progressed from there to two finals. The first, played against Warwickshire at Hartlepool in 1963 was lost 15-9. The second, against Surrey at Twickenham in 1967, ended in a 14-14 draw and was followed by a scoreless replay at Hartlepool. The Championship for that season was then shared between the two counties.

Sunderland's most successful contributor to county rugby during this period was David Boyd who made 38 county appearances. Only legendary England and Lions fly half Mike Weston and fellow international and Lion Johnny Dee gave better service at the time. David, an Ashbrooke man through and through until his tragically early death was educated at St Bees, an established rugby playing school on the Cumberland coast. He represented the county during the successful days of the 50s and 60s and was a back row forward with a well-earned reputation for fearless tackling and determination. West Hartlepool scrum half and future coach Dave Parker still maintains that David Boyd was one of the toughest players he ever faced. Towards the end of the period, Boyd coached the county alongside Mike Weston and was also a county selector. All this, while making major contributions to Sunderland RFC both on and off the field. Such was his value to the club that the announcement of his engagement to be married appeared in the committee minutes!

4.9: *David Boyd at one end and Mike Weston (with ball) at the other - Durham County at Twickenham, 1967*

Hughie Lamb and Bernard Cunningham also made significant contributions to county success. Hughie made over twenty appearances for the county during the latter part of the 'purple patch' (1962-67) and was part of the team which shared the Championship in 1967. Bernard Cunningham was one of those players who lost out to war and continued to give great service locally afterwards. A rugged scrum half, he made nine county appearances between 1949 and 1951. During the war he made an international appearance for England against Wales and seems to have enjoyed his tussle with the great Haydn Tanner during that match. D L Hutton also played for the county between 1953 and 1957 and was chosen to captain the side in the opening friendly against South of Scotland at Ashbrooke during the 1955/6 season. His rugby career was ended by a recurring knee injury.

4.10: Hughie Lamb in Durham kit at Twickenham, 1967

Others who made county appearances just after the war were Tony Greenwell, Robin Auld, E C Douglas, Mike Thompson and S F St Williams. Later appearances were made by Charles Ranken, Ian Hind, Alan Towers, Dave Ritson, A Atkinson and Ted Evans. Towards the end of the period, multi-talented sportsman Chris Storey had begun to take over the mantle formerly worn by Mike Weston. In the late 1960s, a couple of Sunderland players, including Derek Blair, also turned out for Northumberland.

As the growing strength of other counties affected Durham's success in the County Championship, so the gathering strength of Durham clubs started to affect the use of Ashbrooke for county games. Up to the Second World War, Ashbrooke was certainly a leading county ground and, at times the premier county ground. From 1945, its influence began to wane. Immediately after the war, the local derby with Northumberland was played at Ashbrooke. By the late 1960s, the only senior county game played at Sunderland was the annual warm-up for the county season against the Scottish Borders; one memorable game in 1969 ended in a 30-29 defeat for Durham. Few Sunderland players were being capped by the end of the period and, save for the centenary celebrations, the county was making little use of the ground.

Another reason for this decline was the relative lack of spectator interest in rugby in the town. Hartlepool, with a number of rugby clubs and a less successful soccer club, drew bigger crowds to county games and Hartlepool Rovers' ground had become the chosen venue for all County Championship matches by the 1970s. A move to abolish the County Championship in the late 1960s found no support at club or county level.

Off the field of play, Sunderland RFC's input to county rugby was massive and Sunderland officials made highly significant contributions to major initiatives that put the county at the very top of progressive counties (see Appendix Two). Eric Watt Moses, Alan Bean, Hartley Elliott, Robin Auld, Ken Witherington and Harry Keenan were heavily involved in administration, refereeing and coaching; the official photograph of the Durham side that played in the County Championship final at Twickenham in 1967 witnesses this. There are five Sunderland men in the photograph: two players - David Boyd and Hughie Lamb - and three officials - Eric Watt Moses, Alan Bean and Hartley Elliott! (Fred Dale also served as County Honorary Secretary in the mid-1950s.)

There were also a few other significant playing events at Ashbrooke around this time. During the 1966/7 season, the Australian tourists trained at the ground in preparation for their northern matches. Through the good offices of Hartley Elliott, the club also put on a couple of important university matches. One was the UAU Final between Durham and Newcastle (for which the club committee arranged a police presence "as there were likely to be many students"). The English Universities took on the Scottish Universities at Ashbrooke in 1971 and the British Colleges in March 1973.

International Trials

In the decade or so after the war, two international trials were held at Ashbrooke. This is a reflection of the influence at county and international levels of a number the club's administrators. Copies of programmes for both games can be found in the Hartley Elliott file in the club archives.

The international trial held in December 1946 was the first of the season and was refereed by Sunderland RFC's Alan Bean. The two sides were selected as 'The Whites' and 'The Colours' and it is interesting to note the clubs for which the trialists played week in week out. Four played their rugby for London's Saint Mary's Hospital. Waterloo, Bristol, Birkenhead Park and Northampton also had a number of representatives. Of the sides represented, only Bristol and Northampton have enjoyed any real success during the professional era. Local clubs Hartlepool Rovers, Carlisle and Penrith had players in the trial and one of the writers for the programme noted that many playing in the game were "at the start of their fame". Elsewhere in the programme (priced threepence), a short article on the Ashbrooke trial of 1932 informed readers that 21 out of the 30 trialists who appeared that day represented England at some point in their careers.

4.11: 1946 England trial programme

The second trial was held ten years later, almost to the day - in December 1956. On this occasion, it was the second trial of the season and played between the Probables and the Possibles (for a long time this was the most popular form of international trial arrangement). The programme, still priced at threepence, indicated that twelve of the Probables and four of the Possibles had already played for the country. Those readers who were around to enjoy their international rugby in the 1950s will recognise the names of many of the 'greats' of the day. In the Probables, captained by Eric Evans, were Jackson, Butterfield, Bartlett and 'Dickie' Jeeps. One well-known sportsman turning out for the Possibles was M J K Smith, the future England cricket captain. Northampton was well represented again in this trial as were Harlequins, Coventry and both Oxford and Cambridge Universities. A club committee review of the trial concluded that it had been a success although more could have been done in the way of stewarding and press coverage.

PROBABLES
Colours : (White)

1. * D. F. ALLISON (Coventry)

2. * P. B. JACKSON (Coventry)
3. * J. E. BUTTERFIELD (Northampton)
4. * L. B. CANNELL (St. Mary's Hosp'l)
5. * P. H. THOMPSON (Headingley)

6. ‡ R. M. BARTLETT (Harlequins)
7. * R. E. G. JEEPS (Northampton)

8. * C. R. JACOBS (Northampton)
9. * E. EVANS (Captain) Sale
10. * G. W. HASTINGS (Gloucester)
11. ‡ M. R. M. EVANS (Wilmslow)
12. * J. D. CURRIE (Oxford U & Clifton)
13. ‡ A. T. HERBERT (Cambridge U)
14. * A. ASHCROFT (Waterloo)
15. * R. HIGGINS (Liverpool)

4.12: A strong England 'Probables' side at Ashbrooke

Rugby and Soccer

There are signs of continued good relationships between Sunderland RFC and Sunderland AFC in the post-war years. During the early part of the period, the soccer club gained itself the nickname 'The Bank of England Club' and in 1973 won the FA Cup under Bob Stokoe, famously defeating Leeds United by a single goal.

The most interesting contact between the two clubs came in the mid-1950s when SAFC offered to solve the rugby club's pitch problems by taking up a twenty-year lease on the rugby pitch, so junior matches could be played in an enclosure. In return the rugby club was to be offered a soccer club site with two pitches. The proposal was discussed thoroughly (see Appendix One) but nothing came of it. In October 1953 a floodlit match took place at SAFC's Roker Park between a Durham and Northumberland XV - captained by Sunderland's Bernard Cunningham - and Universities' Athletic Union XV. It raised over £400 and a programme stuck in the relevant club minute book reveals that a number of international players were on show. The rugby club's Hartley Elliott refereed the game. One of its aims was to promote the idea of evening floodlit rugby.

The rugby club sent letters of congratulation to the soccer club on a number of occasions including in May 1973. By then, the rugby players had also started to use the soccer club's indoor training facilities at Washington from time to time.

Conclusion

Sunderland RFC reached its centenary in 1973 in pretty good shape on the field of play and, warts and all, still capable of supporting a number of sides at senior and, perhaps more significantly, colt level. It was no longer providing international players and, certainly judging by its fixture list and very average cup performances, was 'one among many' rugby clubs whose players turned out on Saturdays mainly for the fun of the game and the social mix thereafter. These players were probably unaware that within a generation, the face or rugby union was to change in a number of highly significant ways.

Chapter Five
Minis, Juniors, Statics and Leagues (1974-present)

"The rugby section eagerly looks forward to league competition and sees a bright future for the game through the schemes of mini and junior football which they are encouraging."

Ashbrooke Newsletter - December 1986

This useful quotation flags up two of the major developments at Sunderland RFC in recent years - in mini/junior rugby, and in league rugby of the union variety. Equally interesting developments have taken place in connection with players over the age of 35. Observation alone suggests that all three developments have been part of the history of many English rugby clubs in the late twentieth and early twenty-first centuries. Add to this the Rugby Football Union's groundbreaking acceptance of professionalism in the 1990s and we have a game that is very different from that played in earlier times. It is now a happy (or some might argue unhappy) mix of professional, semi-professional and amateur players, and one into which has been added a World Cup, plus various European and National knockout competitions.

Although discussions have taken place over the years about the best role for Sunderland RFC to adopt in the world of modern rugby, today the club remains solidly amateur. This is not to say that money has never changed hands. The story told so far would suggest that there has rarely been any money to change hands yet, for a short period in the late twentieth century and early twenty-first century, a few players and coaches received small sums for their efforts. This was usually as a result of minor outside sponsorship. This practice has now died out and Sunderland RFC like the majority of clubs at its level, is an amateur organisation.

The term 'level' is a key one and perhaps the most important outcome of the introduction of the leagues. When the leagues were formed in the late 1980s, clubs were ranked by the recent achievements of their 1st XV. The process of ranking proved fairly straightforward as the RFU had already approved the reintroduction of the merit tables that had been around in the inter-war years. These had been re-established by the early 1980s. Here teams were positioned according to success against regional rivals and the resultant tables were published in local newspapers.

For Sunderland RFC, the sorting of the leagues came at a bad time, with the 1st XV struggling for results, yet fulfilling a fairly high-status fixture list. Many of the club's age-old opponents seem to have had a similar experience. Quite rightly, history had little part to play in the decisions made over the new leagues and, once placed, the club has moved little from the original level afforded to it almost a quarter of a century ago. Experience teaches that in order to do so, it will need to change its current policy by finding a considerable source of income and by paying a semi-professional wage to most, if not all of its players.

5.1: A programme for the 2010/11 season (note the new kit)

The last three or four decades have been packed with activity at the club both on the field and off, and we are perhaps still too close to this activity to cover it thoroughly or to analyse it fairly. What follows is therefore an overview of what has gone on and what is still going on, based on documents, discussions and personal experience. The true history of this period will have to wait for a later version of the book.

Playing the Game

The years from 1974 to 2011 fall conveniently into two sections, the division coming with the introduction of leagues in 1987

The Dying Days of the Old System (1974-1987)

The standard set by the 1st XV in the centenary season had been a high one and the consensus is that this standard was kept up for the next couple of seasons - with a few reservations. Interest in playing the sport of rugby was still high among older teenagers and adults at Sunderland RFC. Seven sides appeared on Saturdays on a regular basis including an extra 4th XV and a Colts B side which was formed to encourage those about to leave school.

By the mid-1970s, the annual match with the Dolphins had become a fixture and the Dolphins an official RFU club based at Ashbrooke. Tony Butlin, Sunderland RFC coach in the mid-1970s, introduced a strict training regime which included gym work. The 1977/8 season with a tough fixture list was considered a satisfactory one as both the 1st XV and 2nd XV achieved the magical 50%-plus success rate. In 1978, the new Northern Merit Table was introduced and Sunderland RFC's 1st XV was not part of it. The secretary for the previous season noted with pride that the team had managed to defeat a number of sides due to enter this league but 1978 seems to have been something of a watershed. During the following season, the 1st XV recorded only eight wins in 31 games and no other Sunderland side made 50%.

As noted previously, the fixture list at this time was a tough one. It included John Player Cup winners Gosforth, Kendal, Middlesborough, Jedforest, Haddington, Hull and East Riding, Edinburgh Academicals, Oxford Univeristy and Jordanhill. In the 1980 game with Jordanhill the 1st XV front row came across the legendary 'Mighty Mouse' Mclauchlan - an unforgettable experience.

5.2: A 1st XV from the 1970s

The 1980s began very nervously. The minutes reveal committee members contemplating the 'likelihood of a league system in five years or so', and being keen to improve so Sunderland RFC could "enjoy a proud playing record as a 1st class club". Sadly the club hit an all-time low in the early 1980s. There was a visible decline in its fortunes that matched the downturn in the local economy where shipbuilding and coal mining were in their death throes. At first, playing numbers remained high but, with the exception of a "reasonable" 1980/1 season, the writing was on the wall. By November 1982, the 1st XV had only recorded two wins in 13 games. It was a bad season all round despite the magnificent efforts of captain Tommy Harrison. Only eight victories were recorded with numerous injuries, the loss of promising youngsters and the cancellation of the dinner dance all adding to the doom and gloom. This was not dispelled when the two sides due to visit on Easter tours pulled out at the last minute. By Christmas 1983, only three out of 16 1st XV games had been won although the 4th XV was doing well under the guidance of committee man Steve Harrison. In a poor season all round, the 1st XV won only 11 out of its 37 games.

Worse still, the decline was there for all to see in the form of the local Journal Merit Table. Here the 1st XV was frequently close to the bottom of the 'league' and at one point near to the foot of its 2nd Division. It was not what was needed and, as one committee member remarked in the early 1980s, "at the present time there is a lot of talk about leagues and status etc and the position to say the least is very difficult. We must take action now if we are not to lose out in these possible changes".

The desired improvement was not forthcoming. A "disastrous" 1982/3 season saw only eight 1st XV victories and, after a brief recovery, the 1985/6 season proved equally unsuccessful. By now the club was without a coach which put a great deal of strain on the shoulders of captain Dave Hodgson. It was also struggling to find a 3rd XV and started the following season without one. In the season prior to the formation of the leagues, the 1st XV recorded only six wins.

Despite poor results on the pitch, the club spirit remained high with successful Easter tours in England and on the continent and a continuity of off the pitch social events.

The League Era (1987 to present)

The league system has been in existence for almost a quarter of a century and has been nipped and tucked from time to time. Today it consists of a pyramid of 12 levels. The top five levels are described as national and the top two leagues are professional. The vast bulk of rugby in the country is now played at regional/local level with Sunderland RFC's 1st XV 'one among many', as it has played at levels 6 to 9 since the leagues were introduced in 1987. For the last few seasons the team has played at level 7 and, in the 2011/12 season, faces age-old rivals in this division including Hartlepool Rovers, Darlington, Stockton, Ryton, Medicals and Novocastrians. Like Sunderland RFC these are clubs with lengthy histories and proud heritage.

The leagues in Sunderland's area have been divided into North East (higher) and Durham and Northumberland (lower). Sunderland is currently in Durham and Northumberland 1. It started life in Durham and Northumberland 2, and also dabbled in the lower reaches of the North Eastern leagues for a few seasons.

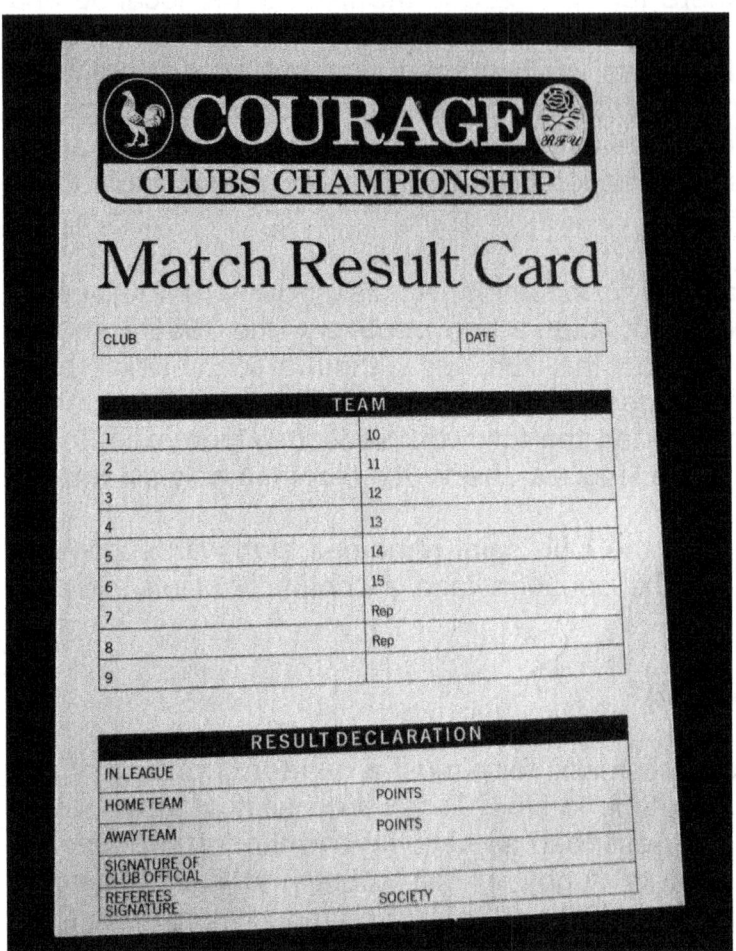

5.3: Into the leagues

Initial success came in 1988/9, the second league season, when the 1st XV, under captain Jim Smith, ran away with Durham and Northumberland 2, losing only one league match and scoring a large number of points. The committee saw this as "only the very beginning of a process to put Sunderland back in the best of north east rugby". While acknowledging the success, it was noted that the opposition was generally weaker than that faced in the last few seasons under the old system.

Another period of interest came early in the 21st century when the 1st XV was relegated to Durham and Northumberland 3, at level 9 - the lowest level at which the club has ever played. This happened in 2004 and the following few seasons, under Chairman Andy Kyle, saw a determined effort to move onwards and upwards. The club drew up a long-term plan and the 1st XV recorded consecutive promotions, ending up in Northumberland and Durham 1. In the club's single season in Northumberland and Durham 3, where they were still encountering old rivals such as Medicals and Whitley Bay, the side scored 423 points against 92 and came within a whisker of being one of *Rugby World's* teams of the season. At the end of the 2006/7 season, the 1st XV lost a home play-off to York due to a last minute try; victory would have meant promotion to North East 2.

The 1st XV played in the North East Leagues in the 1990s and many of the players found match arrangements difficult. These leagues spread down into Yorkshire and brought the club into contact with teams in the Leeds and Bradford area. With a changing economic environment some of the players had to work night shifts and found both the travel and even the playing itself to be challenging. Rob Stormont, former club captain and current mini rugby coach, noted in 1998 that the league system had to some extent turned his 'hobby' into a form of 'job'. "Surely this is not what it's all about," he wrote in the club's 125th anniversary newsletter. Today (and still playing for the 3rd XV) he accepts that league competitiveness had put a good edge on the game and that the club's current top Northumberland and Durham league status probably reflects the type of fixture list the club might have had under the old system.

Among all this, the Easter tours continued and most enjoyable (and in some cases unreportable) visits were made to the Lake District and West Cumbria.

Minis and Juniors

The first inkling that the club might invest permanently in sides younger than colt age came in the early 1970s when Neville Boyd informed the club committee that Hartlepool Old Boys were experimenting with 'mini colts'. In 1972, Westoe offered to play Sunderland at this level but there was no club interest at this stage. By 1973, there was a sense of urgency and moves were made to start a side for children in the first year at secondary school (under 12 age group). Their parents had to be club members. In the same year an under 15 and an under 17 side from Sunderland took part in the Darlington Schoolboys' Festival. Games for younger schoolboys were also arranged for the school holidays during the mid to late 1970s. Intriguingly one of the main concerns about starting 'mini rugby' was that the youngsters might stray into the Ashbrooke bar on Sunday lunchtimes and cost the club its licence.

This early mini rugby was under the watchful eyes of Hughie Lamb and Keith Winlow and there was talk of Ashbrooke becoming one of three centres for mini county tournaments. By the end of the decade all this seems to have fizzled out.

As the opening quotation suggests, the revival of mini rugby came at the same time as the introduction of the leagues and understandably so. With poor senior results in the early 1980s and a long-term league life likely, rebuilding from the bottom seemed the best option. The move to mini and junior rugby has been generally successful with many, if not most, of the senior players today having passed through these sections. In 2008, 50% of the 1st and 2nd XV had come through the mini/junior system and the club has to thank former captain Ian Hind for putting the impetus into mini/ midi rugby (under 7s to under 12s). He was in charge from 1987-1993 and was followed by Keith Gregson, Mandy Wright, Paul Geehan, Kevin Hazard and John Buddington. Former 1st XV player Peter Nicholson also looked after junior rugby for a number of years.

Over the years mini and junior rugby (up to the age of 16) has consisted of regular coaching in individual and unit skills plus friendlies, occasional tours and competitions. Of these competitions, the County Cup has been the most valued and the club has enjoyed success here across the years. In the 1993/4 season, Sunderland RFC won three of the four County Cups (under 9, under 10 and under 11). The under 10 team from that season - coached by former player Stu Hutchinson and later by John Tate - was to become one of the most successful sides in the club's history.

Between 1993 and 2000, the under 10 side of 1993/4 won the County Cup on six occasions and also enjoyed success at significant regional festivals held at Darlington, Houghton, Kirkby Lonsdale and Blyth. Peter Harrison, Danny Thompson, Mark Wilson and John Gregson later played for the club's 1st XV while full back Jon Cloak and Michael Tate moved to league rugby elsewhere. The team, however, failed to advance to colt level as a result of injuries and the demands of work and senior schoolboy rugby.

The under 9 side from the same season produced two internationals - Ben Simpson who played fly half for England Schools, and Peter Phelan who was scrum half in a number of Irish national junior sides. He spent some time with Newcastle Falcons and in the Irish leagues, and was featured in *Rugby World* magazine as a 'hotshot'. Eventually he moved into semi-professional rugby.

5.4: County Cup success for a junior side of the 1990s

The under 11s of 1993/4 had also won the cup the previous season and one of its stars was Laura Stockdale, who later went to the United States on a soccer scholarship (another young female player, Laura Elphinstone, moved into acting and has appeared on television and on the London stage). Also in this side was Tom Hirst, destined to become a brave, battered and bruised stalwart of the club for years to come plus loyal and long-serving prop Richard 'Sparrow' Arrowsmith; also future senior Liam Collins and international Nick Hooper. Nick was a talented all-round sportsman who played for England Schools and had a professional career with Newcastle Falcons put on permanent hold due to injury. He still turned out for Sunderland 1st XV in the centres during the early 21st century.

The under 10 side of 1995 reached the final of the County Cup only to come across Westoe and Katy McLean. Westoe won the final due to the hard tackling of this young lady who is now England Ladies' fly half and captain. The Sunderland side, generally small and young in age, stuck together for barren season after barren season until, still together and experienced, they won every game at an under 17 international tournament in Holland. From this side Brian

Finlay, James Kyle, Paul Gregson and Luke Robinson went on to play 1st XV rugby for Sunderland.

5.5: Katy McLean, future England captain, in action against Sunderland under 10s

From the same era came a crop of minis who advanced to the seniors under the watchful eye of coach Ian Horner. In this crop were fly half Ian Dobson, forward Andrew Hall and club captain Peter Carter. From the same side Jonathan Boatman is currently captain of West Hartlepool at Level 5, and has two sporting brothers who also started as Ashbrooke minis.

An earlier success was enjoyed by the under 12 County Cup winning side during the 1990/1 season. This team won further cups in 1993 and 1994 and lost the 1995 final. They were unbeaten during the 1990/1 season. The team's captain, James Lofthouse later captained a grand-slam winning England under 18 side from number 10, with Jonny Wilkinson at inside centre. He enjoyed a brief career in professional rugby at Bath and Worcester and succeeded in both county and university rugby before injury forced him to call it a day. A number of players from the 1990/1 side represented county schools and clubs, north schools and England schools. Neil Gale and Robbie Harrison later played for Sunderland 1st XV while Martin Watt was 1st XV captain in the 2010/11 season and still plays with prop Alan Ross, a North of England schools' player who started in the same mini side. Mini and junior half back Tom Gregson was the eldest of three brothers who won silverware at the club.

Around the millennium, a successful under 12 side took the County Cup under coach Paul Geehan. From this side, Chris Geehan, Jamie McLennan and Sean Bellon went on to play for the 1st XV.

The minis and juniors enjoyed a number of tours over the years. These took them to Ireland, Scotland, France, Holland and the Midlands, and one group had the pleasure of playing on pitches at Rugby School. The youngsters have also enjoyed coaching sessions organised by Newcastle Falcons.

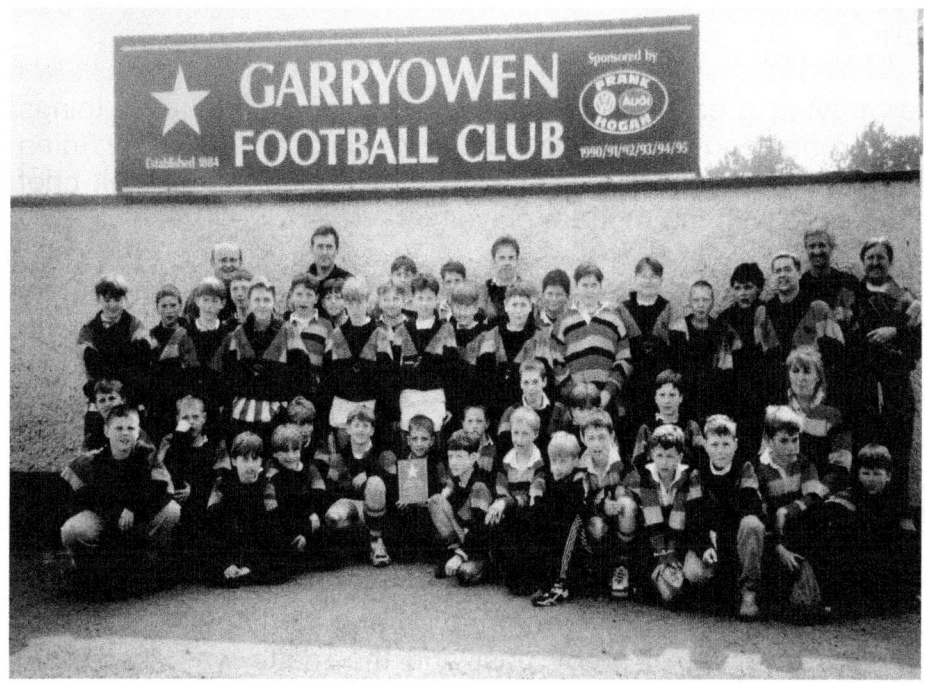

5.6: Minis and juniors enjoy some excellent Irish hospitality in the 1990s

In the mid-1980s, the club secretary wrote of his delight at "over 50 kids in club colours on a Sunday morning". By 1987/8 Ian Hind was organising five mini sides and teams at junior level from under 13 to under 16. This 'section' of the rugby club was also self-funding and teams were coached by enthusiastic non-rugby parents and experienced ex-playing parents such as Peter McCarron,

Chris Storey and Frank Greenshields. In 1998, with Mandy Wright at the helm (mother of sons who advanced to senior rugby), forty adults and two hundred youngsters were involved in this form of rugby at Ashbrooke on a regular basis.

In his programme notes for the 2010/11 season, club captain Peter Carter, himself a former mini, noted that the mini and junior rugby was "bearing fruit". This is likely to continue to be the case with current and former players now involved in every side from under 7 to under 16.

In common with other clubs around its level, Sunderland RFC has lost promising youngsters to semi-professional and professional clubs at higher levels. A number of these have returned to the club after a couple of unhappy seasons 'warming the bench' elsewhere - not the most rewarding experience either for player or club.

Statics and Seniors

While the club was paying great attention to its youngsters, intriguing things were going on at the other end of the age range. In Victorian and Edwardian times players of 35 and over were generally looking toward the end of their brief career. This is not the case with the modern player.

The first stirrings of 'very senior' rugby came about in the late twentieth century with the formation of Sunderland Statics under the watchful eye of Yorkshireman Paul Sturgess. Since opposition was not hard to find it is fairly safe to assume that this was part of a wider trend. Although players continued to take the game seriously, some fun was had in naming these sides. In nearby Hartlepool, for example, one team decided to call itself the Euthanasians. As for Sunderland Statics, Paul Sturgess noted in a 1987 match programme that the qualifications for playing were to "have a pulse; to be over 35 and to have played rugby for the club at some point". The team turned out once a month and had its own (yellow) shirt with a badge and a motto. This badge portrayed an elderly gentleman with a stick standing in front of a set of rugby post and the motto was 'ludendum laetitia super omnium', which has something to do with playing for fun above all else. With this in mind it is hardly surprising to find regular tours a popular entry on the Statics' calendar.

Tony Markham, a long-term player who also became heavily involved in the administration of the rugby club and wider Ashbrooke club, has clear memories of Statics' rugby. He says that it was surprisingly competitive with a number of rivalries dating back to colts' level emerging out of the woodwork. He also notes that many sides delighted in trying to turn the Statics over as the club as a whole still had a reputation as being one of the 'posher' ones in the region. This was something that Tony, a Midlander by birth, failed to understand as the teams in which he played at Ashbrooke included men and youngsters from all walks of life.

The Statics eventually died the death for a positive reason. By the end of the twentieth century many players over 35 still wanted to play competitive rugby on a weekly basis at least into their 40s and in some cases beyond. Serious sports historians, psychologists and medical historians will undoubtedly combine their researches to decide why; extended longevity and improved health through a decline in both smoking and heavy manual labour must be in the frame here (although we must draw a veil over the subject of excessive alcohol consumption). In addition, the desire to continue sporting relationships on the field and social relationships off it must come under consideration. Many of the current 3rd XV belong to this age group and, in a number of cases, players have played together in a variety of senior sides for twenty years and more. By combining with youngsters fresh from the colts they offer the club a useful blend of youth and experience. In the first decade of the twenty-first century, the 3rd XV secured the local 3rd team league thanks to the efforts of the '600 club', i.e., a team with so many of an age that the total reached the 600 year mark. In November 2008 a squad of 24 turned up to take on Mowden Park 3rd XV with an entire fifteen with experience at 1st XV level from the 1970s onwards, plus a father and son.

As current club chairman Paul Geehan notes wryly, he cannot get any 'old f—ts' to run the club as nobody wants to be an 'old f—t'; those of advanced years are too busy playing the game. Quite a turnaround!

Colts Rugby

Throughout the modern period, the club has continued to target the important 16-18 age group - with mixed results. The introduction of comprehensive education in the early 1970s tended to decrease the amount of school rugby played by youngsters of this age. However the old grammar schools and public schools continued to play the game and increasingly regulations were introduced to prevent players within this system from playing for clubs at the same time. In a number of cases in the 1990s, the club was unable to turn successful junior sides into colts' sides as a result.

In general, the club's success at senior level often matched earlier success at colt level and coaches (many of them secondary teachers themselves) were able to draw on pupils from new local comprehensives Southmoor, St. Aidan's, Red House and Monkwearmouth. Brother followed brother and friend followed friend into the colts' side and from time to time a junior colts was also in operation. A programme from a 1984 St Aidan's School v Old Boys game shows a number of members of the successful 1988/9 side club 1st XV playing for both sides. Both Brother O' Brien and Paddy McConville from this school are remembered fondly for their coaching and encouragement.

The colts enjoyed a good spell in the mid-1970s under Hughie Lamb and Alan Towers and made it to consecutive County Cup finals although they ended on the losing side in both cases. There were games with local rivals Belford House for the Otterson Trophy, and in 1982 the Junior Colts were successful in their County Cup. A number of the colts were chosen to play for the county including Gary Davison, David Lindsley, Paul Davis, Sean Crawley and Keith Reay. Adrian Kelf was another significant colt who captained the side well and went on to give service to the 1st XV. Kevin Pyle, a promising fly half, was chosen for the county at under 19 level.

The least satisfactory periods for colts rugby came when the senior sides were weak and short of players. This was particularly true in the 1980s when colts were moved into these sides to make up the numbers when they were not quite ready. They also lacked the support of more seasoned players to help them through the experience, although former colt Jamie Boyd found the experience "character building" - especially when he was called upon to mark future England winger Chris Oti.

Today, colts' rugby is thriving thanks to the enthusiasm of coach Clive Fish and the club hopes to benefit as a result. More and more young players at senior colts' level and above are staying locally for their further education due to the economic downturn and pressure of fees. In some cases they are already settled with other local clubs but there can be little doubt that Sunderland RFC has benefited from this trend. In the past the movement of youngsters to universities and colleges some distance away has been to the club's disadvantage.

County and National Cup Competitions

The Durham Senior Challenge Cup is still in existence but its organisation has changed over the years in order to match other changes in the structure of rugby. At the same time, national competitions have been introduced at different levels and these have created considerable local interest from time to time.

The disappearance of the categories 'senior' and 'junior' with rugby clubs has had its effect on the different County Cups. With a mere scattering of local clubs in the national leagues and just below, cup competition at the top level has been very limited and has not been a club's priority. Sunderland 1st XV failed to win the former Senior Challenge Cup during this period although it did reach the final in the 1990s only to lose to a strong Stockton side. The 2nd XV reached the finals in 1975 and 2008; firstly it was defeated by Durham City and in then by Blaydon whose 1st XV was then playing in the national leagues. In 1980, the 3rd XV made the County Cup final and lost to Hartlepool Rovers 13-6.

While playing in the Durham and Northumberland Leagues, the 1st XV have qualified for the former junior trophy now called the Durham County Challenge Cup. Here the side has enjoyed success, particularly in the early years of the twenty-first century taking the trophy in 2004, 2005 and 2006. The 2004 victory was over Winlaton Vulcans and the 2005 over Seaton Carew. The 2006 final victory was over Bishop Auckland by 43-0 with Rob Stormont the successful captain and fine displays from Matt Goforth, Richie Holborough and Tony Irwin. The 2007 final was, however, lost to Ryton.

Like the county competitions, the relatively new national competitions can be a little confusing. On some occasions, entry to these competitions has been through selection and at other times through winning a local trophy or by reaching a particular league position. As a result of its County Cup final appearance in 1996, the 1st XV qualified for the first round of rugby's equivalent of the FA Cup - the Pilkington Trophy. The draw took them across to Kendal, a strong side on the fringes of the Lake District, and also to an inevitable early exit from the competition.

On two occasions in the early twenty first century, the 1st XV has made good progress in the national Powergen Vase, on one occasion coming close to a final at Twickenham. In the 2004/5 season, an unexpected 13-12 away victory over Yorkshire club Ripon in the 3rd round was followed by a 25-6 home victory over Liverpool-based Sefton. The 5th round tie away to old rivals from Manchester Heaton Moor ended in a narrow loss. The game was played in appalling conditions with a chance to win in the last minute going begging as penalty opportunities disappeared in the glutinous mud. In 2006, Sunderland reached the last 16 of the competition and lost away to Shropshire club Cleobury Mortimer 17-12. At one point Sunderland was ahead by 12 points to 7 but fell behind after a player was sent off. The Shropshire side advanced to Twickenham where they were losing finalists.

Other trophies contested in this period include the Vaux Sampson Shield and the annual Ryton 15-a-side Festival Trophy. The first was a competition held at Ashbrooke in the latter years of the twentieth century and entered mostly by junior clubs. Sunderland took this trophy on a number of occasions. The Ryton tournament is held before the start of the league season and attracts a number of sides around Sunderland's 1st XV level. Again success has been achieved in this competition in recent years.

The cup successes are both heartening and good for club spirits although many players and officials acknowledge a desire to perform and succeed at slightly higher levels in the future.

The success of mini and junior teams in their various cup competitions is dealt with in the appropriate sections.

Sevens

Sevens rugby has grown in stature in recent years. It is now a fast-moving Olympic sport with well-supported national and international competitions. Sunderland RFC has shown more interest in the shorter game in this period than at any time since the 1930s.

From the 1970s onwards, teams were entered for competitions on a regular basis and the occasional trophy won. In the 1974/5 season, five sevens competitions were entered and the final of the Northumberland sevens lost to Wigton.

From time to time, the club has enjoyed success in the Durham City Sevens known as the 'Town and Gown' due to its university links. The side that won the 1996 Durham City Sevens had fast backs in Micky Simpson, Steve Graham, Richie Reah and Jamie Boyd, big boots with Graham Towers and Graham Waddell and mobile forwards in Tony Irwin and Andy Black.

Sevens activity tends to take place when a group of friends decide to give it a go and after competitions the feeling was that more could have been achieved. Ashbrooke has always had a reputation for its backs' play and for mobile intelligent forwards. Sevens suits this style of play yet over the years, the committee has reflectively bemoaned what might have been on the sevens' front with further 'practice' and 'preparation'

Players and Coaches

This is potentially the most difficult chapter of the book to write as so many players have pulled on a Sunderland shirt over the last four decades and most of them are still around to question a lack of reference to them in the club's history. Clearly there is not space to mention one and all so what follows is a representative list of captains and coaches as well as some influential players and a few colourful characters with humble apologies to everybody else. Many of those not mentioned below are referred to elsewhere in this chapter.

5.7: A strong league 1st XV from the 1990s

The club has been blessed with a number of captains who have led by example during this period including Dave Hodgson, Brian Green, Graham Edmundson, and Tony Irwin. Tommy Harrison, one of the club's greatest stalwarts, led the 1st XV through the dark days of the 1980s and still turns out to play and referee in the second decade of the twenty-first century. Jim Smith, an inspirational leader whose career was halted early through injury, led the 1st XV to success in the early days of league rugby and formed a formidable second row partnership with the late Ian Herbert (see dedication of the book). Rob Stormont attracted the utmost respect as captain. Once a full back, he recovered from a horrific injury to lead the 1st XV in the successful seasons of the twenty-first century from the back row. His knowledge of the game is currently being shared with the youngest of the club's mini players. In the 2010/11 season he coached the under 8s. Peter Carter, a mini in the 1990s, has steadied the ship in recent years and gives his thoughts on the game on a regular basis in the match programme.

5.8: Jim Smith leading from the top of the lineout

The club has also seen a number of coaches in this period although it remained 'coachless' during some of its darker days. Coaches include Ian Stafford, Dave

Hodgson, Paul Davis, Graham Young and Harry Wilson. The current long-serving coach is Frazer Kennedy who has been influential both as player and coach in the early twenty-first century. Blooded in the Scottish leagues with Currie, he works professionally with the rugby players at Newcastle University and brings a vast amount of rugby know-how to the club.

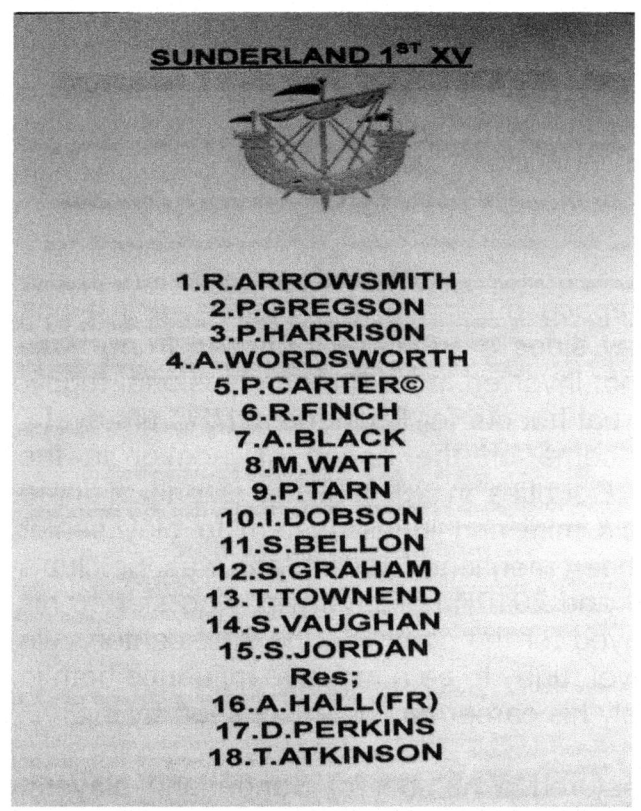

SUNDERLAND 1ST XV

1.R.ARROWSMITH
2.P.GREGSON
3.P.HARRISON
4.A.WORDSWORTH
5.P.CARTER©
6.R.FINCH
7.A.BLACK
8.M.WATT
9.P.TARN
10.I.DOBSON
11.S.BELLON
12.S.GRAHAM
13.T.TOWNEND
14.S.VAUGHAN
15.S.JORDAN
Res;
16.A.HALL(FR)
17.D.PERKINS
18.T.ATKINSON

5.9: A recent 1st XV packed with former minis and juniors

The list of influential players covering forty years is endless. Success has often come thanks to a big boot and, in this respect, Graham Waddell, John Grainger, Chris Storey, Michael Porter, Graham Towers, Sean Bellon and Ian Dobson deserve to be mentioned. On the longevity front, homage should be paid to Tony Watt, Eddie Collins, Dale Wilkinson, Micky Brace, Peter Roseberry, Andy Black and Ed Bengochea. Ed is a tireless team manager who started as a colt at the very beginning of this period and continued to serve the club as hooker season after season. Simpson and Jackson were not a firm of tailors but a devastating combination of wingmen. Richie Reah, a Scottish schoolboy international via boarding school, was nippy in the centres as was Mel Stoker, Jamie Boyd son of flanker David, a reliable winger and full back, and Ian Towers son of Alan, another reliable back. Alan Hughes, a back whose career was ended by injury, moved in to be a respected referee and international line judge. Seasoned campaigners such as Harry Parlett did fine work with sides below 1st XV level while a few players such as Richie Holborough, Matt Goforth, Ian Dalton and Steve Dembry left their mark on the club during short stays.

Typical of the club perhaps is Kev Logan who was a pupil at Southmoor School in 1978 when his brother asked him to turn up for the colts when the side was a man short. He has rarely been out of the club since and has played for and supported the club in a number of vital capacities.

County and Other Representation

The County Championship rolls on apace but in the professional era it has become a very different animal. Today sides are generally chosen from those players at levels 3, 4 and 5 who are not involved in full-time professional rugby. Under these circumstances it was a great honour for Sunderland RFC at Level 7 to have Peter Harrison chosen to come off the bench as hooker in the championship game against Eastern Counties in 2011. Peter is one of three brothers who came through the club's mini and junior system to play senior rugby (only scrum half David has not been mentioned so far), and was the club's Player of the Season in both 2009/10 and 2010/11. Tony Irwin, who started his career at the club as a youngster, played for the county in the 21st century. He returned to Sunderland from higher level rugby to be a massive influence both in set pieces and loose play. Unfortunately his career has been cut short by injury.

In the 1970s County Durham still featured a number of Sunderland players. Among these was Charlie Bentley, possibly the club's most successful player during the latter part of the twentieth century. A giant lineout man, Charlie was singled out for praise in many of his county and club matches. In the 1978/9 season his display for Durham against Lancashire and England captain Bill Beaumont attracted particular attention. A fine captain and coach, Charlie eventually moved to West Hartlepool along with fellow Sunderland player Graham Young. Here both played for a club, which was then one of the leading ones in the country. Chris Storey continued to appear as fly half while the promising John Nicholson, one of the stars of Sunderland's 1973/4 1st XV made a number of appearances as scrum half. Colin Foster also played at county level prior to his move to Canada.

The senior county has rarely played at Ashbrooke during the period, the Durham v Cumbria match of 1984 being reported as "a rare honour for the club". During the 1981/2 season Durham County hosted the Scottish Borders at the ground while the British and Scottish Colleges clashed there a few years earlier. The county schools and other junior county sides have also played here on occasions.

Many of the youngsters playing at the club represented county clubs and county schools during this period with some of the more successful sides having half a dozen players or more in a county squad at one time. In the early days, Peter Lillington was prominent at county youth and Scottish Schools' level. Today Guy Kingsley-Smith has been in the county schools' squad and has had his talent monitored by Newcastle Falcons.

Pitches

After more than a century, the age-old question of the pitch (or pitches) runs on apace although now there appears to be a light at the end of the tunnel.

The Ashbrooke pitch continued to cause problems in the late twentieth century despite frequent work on it, and it often fell victim to the weather. It had a tendency to flood and drainage proved a constant problem and one which, in past years, has been partly responsible for the loss of senior county fixtures. Thankfully the problems seem to be under control today

The original Ryhope Road pitches have now gone. The rugby club had a constant battle to keep them in playable condition and found itself stuck between the devil and the deep blue sea, needing somewhere outside Ashbrooke to play but generally unhappy with the arrangement despite the valiant efforts of various groundsmen. In 1977 when the pitches themselves were playable the committee minutes refered to "increasing use of the ground by trespassers; its very fine condition acting as an incentive to use it for purposes ranging from horse-riding to walking the dog".

Eventually economic necessity decreed that the ground be sold for housing and this happened in two phases (see Appendix One). The first phase, in the 1980s, saw the ground reduced to a single pitch with housing on the rest. Complaints about what remained were frequent in the 1990s and eventually the remainder was sold for housing in the first decade of the current century. The search went on for an alternative ground but this proved difficult and the old questions of distance and a potentially divided sports club reared their ugly heads.

In the meantime, the club has had to do with the hiring of a council pitch at Hillview - a good twenty minutes' walk to the south-west of Ashbrooke. All senior teams have played here at one time or another and it is well used for junior and colt matches too. The pitch, surrounded by football pitches, is on a slope and, as the name suggests, within view of one of Sunderland's Tunstall Hills. The ground is rather exposed causing problems for players and spectators alike and attracting the well-worn moan, "We're not at Hillview are we?!" The close proximity of housing also causes problems and one committee minute of the late twentieth century listed the particular houses, greenhouses and conservatories which kickers were to avoid where possible.

School facilities at nearby Southmoor School have also been used for mini and junior rugby from time to time as were the playing fields at a former school a couple of miles to the west. These playing fields have now been turned over to housing.

More recently the wider club has purchased the site of a former creamery further out on the Ryhope Road. This site is still under development and it is very much a case of 'watch this space'. All the old problems of distance and protection of the site are present as is the fear that setting up facilities on a large-scale basis may eventually lead to a 'divorce' from the mother club at Ashbrooke. Sharing this new ground with another sport or educational organisation may, in time, solve the problems. Meanwhile after considerable preparatory work, the new pitch is now ready for playing rugby.

The Committee

The rugby club committee remains an important part of the club although the league system has taken away much of the work from the fixtures' secretary. The entertainment sub-committee also retains the important task of seeing that the club is funded. Organised dances, raffles and dinners continue to be an element in this and occasional sponsorship has also proved very useful. During the 2004/5 season, sale of Christmas Raffle tickets was linked to the payment of some of the players' membership fees.

In the early 1980s, the season's cost amounted to around £2,000. By the 1992/3 season it had reached almost £4,000. Two-thirds of this went on food and transport while almost 50% was raised by subscriptions, plus 30% through raffles and a regular draw. Sponsorship accounted for around 20% of income.

In many cases the talk was still of a hand to mouth existence and the main aim of fundraising was simply to cover the season's expenses. The chief outlay has been on food and transport and the costs of both rose dramatically in the early 1970s with the massive rise in oil prices.

Among the people who have worked tirelessly for the committee during this time are a number of former players including Mick Wood, Tony Markham, Tony Watt, Steve Thompson, Alan Towers, John Martin, Harry Wilson and the Boyd brothers - Neville and David. Adam Scott Gray who played for the club in the pre-war years was still involved in the arrangement of fixtures in the 1980s. The entertainment committee work of Dave Hodgson, Keith Reay, Steve Harrison and Kev Logan is also worthy of praise.

The redoubtable Jimmy Lee finally retired in 1980 having served the club as player, organiser, steward and groundsman for over thirty years. He was presented with a cheque in excess of £1,000 and was described at the time as "the sort of man that makes a rugby club tick".

Epilogue - The 2011 AGM

The writing of a book such as this necessitates trawling through year after year of AGMs so it was intriguing, in the light of this, to attend the 2011 AGM with a head full of history and an open mind. The meeting proved a very positive affair and future prospects on the whole seem good.

Although the 1st XV slid down the league towards the end of the season, it was generally agreed that the side had enjoyed its rugby, as had most of the senior sides. The main problems came as a result of a series of injuries and the disruption caused to training and games by the harsh winter. The general feeling is that the club could survive at the next level without changing its current philosophy.

The 2nd XV struggled in the Candy League where it was coming across sides connected to teams with 1st XVs playing at much higher levels. The decision was thus taken to leave the league and set up more suitable fixtures. With a few victories under its belt, the side began to settle down, develop and to take on new players. In the 2011/12 season both the 2nd XV and 3rd XV play in the Northumberland Leagues against many old rivals of a similar standard. It should be noted that an added attraction of league games will be a post-match stop off in the fleshpots of Newcastle on the way home from away fixtures - something much enjoyed (if poorly recalled) in the past.

The colts have also been developing well and, with the ever-changing financial climate, many are expected to stay at home which should benefit the club over the next few years. Mini and junior sides operated from under 7s to under 16s with coaches qualified and checked under the new stringent RFU arrangements. This is proving a particularly fruitful time, as a number of the coaches played in the most successful sides of the league period and are now passing on their knowledge to their own children and their friends. In 1881 Sunderland's senior XV won the first County Cup; in 2011 the club's under 7 side came out top in highly competitive RFU-sponsored regional competition!

The 2011 AGM also provides some indication of the way in which the running of the club has changed in some ways yet remained the same in others. The committee is now smaller and has a female secretary in Gillian Geehan, another tireless worker over the years at mini, junior and senior level. Its chairman, Paul Geehan, previously organised mini and junior rugby, while the treasurer is seasoned and long-serving ex-captain Tommy Harrison. Interested parties are invited onto the committee which has only one business meeting a month (the selection committee meets weekly during the season). Funding is dependent on a small sponsorship and funds raised from events organised by both the rugby club and the wider Ashbrooke club. The current sponsors are solicitors Sweeney Miller, a local business appropriately working out of one of Ashbrooke's Victorian villas.

In the 2010/11 season, £24,000 was needed and raised. As ever, that leaves little in the way of slack for buying kit or equipment and the collection of membership fees remains an issue. In these last two cases, 'twas ever thus.

And Finally...

In the 2010/11 season and before embarking on much of the research for this book, I wrote the following introduction for the season's match programme:

"In many ways Sunderland RFC or 'Ashbrooke' as it is sometimes known is a good old-fashioned English rugby club and pleased to be seen as such. Rugby is played as much for pleasure as success (although success is not unimportant). Spirits are high among the players and in a world where dour professionalism is often the order of the day, a few glasses are raised round the club to the spirit and enjoyment of the finest of English sports."

After twelve months of discussion and further archive-delving, I have discovered little, if anything, to change this view.

Appendix

The decision to have a lengthy appendix is a deliberate one. The main aim of this book is to tell the story of Sunderland RFC, a rugby club that is 'one among many'. While material for the book was being collected, it became clear that the story was throwing up a number of interesting side-issues, which were in danger of clogging up the main tale. Thus the decision was made to look at these separately.

The most important of these issues (Appendix One) relates to the rugby club's role as a section of the wider Ashbrooke Sports Club. Although in an appendix to the main body of the book, this is still essential reading for anybody keen to understand the workings of what is a rare survival from Victorian times.

Appendix Two contains the biographies of a number of the rugby club administrators who have left their mark on the wider world of rugby while still heavily involved with their parent club.

The final appendix (Appendix Three) examines the subject of the all-round sportsman and poses questions about his changing roles across the years.

Appendix One
'One Among Many' - the Rugby Section of the Wider Sports Club (1887 to date)

"Ashbrooke is a large and complex club' It is a credit to all concerned that the various sections manage to co-exist as well as they do"

Rugby section annual report, 1980

In 1895, the Sunderland Cricket and Rugby Football Club organised a Grand Bazaar. In celebration of the event, somebody wrote the following song to the tune 'John Peel', and dedicated it to the club's 'overworked secretary'.

WE KEN OUR TEAM WITH THE YELLOW AND THE BLACK
AND THE RED STRIPE TOO ON EVERY STURDY BACK
THOUGH OUT BANKING ACCOUNT LOOKS TERRIBLY SLACK
OUR BAZAAR'LL PUT IT RIGHT IN THE MORNING

Do you ken the lads who at Ashbrooke play?
Do you ken the lads in the stripey array?
They're going to push the Rovers right away
When they meet them in the final in the morning

Do you also ken our cricketing lads?
With their deep dug blocks and other little fads
And the ball that yorks them off their pads
Yet they're Champions of the League in the morning

Do you ken the lads who love to trick
Opponents on the field with a spring-handled stick
And to black each other's eyes with a ball like a brick
And they call it 'Playing Hockey' in the morning

Do you ken the lads with the nice refrain
Of 'Very nice length – hard lines again'
Who shout out 'Narrer' in the pouring rain
And earn a nice sore throat for the morning

The song neatly sums up why this book needs at least one added chapter. The story of Sunderland RFC does not stand alone even in regard to the very ground on which the club has played for nearly 125 years. Sunderland RFC may be 'one among many' as a typical rugby playing club; it is also one among many sporting sections of the wider Ashbrooke Sports Club (formerly Sunderland Cricket and Football Club).

Rugby and the Other Sports

Cricket had been played in Sunderland since the time of the Napoleonic Wars and modern sports historians now recognise the Sunderland Cricket Club as the oldest documented sporting club in the Tyne and Wear area, dateable to 1834. Once established at Ashbrooke, Sunderland CC became a major force in regional cricket especially after the setting up of the Durham Senior League towards the end of the Victorian period. The cricket club's 1st XI topped the league on a number of occasions and in 2000 it became the first side to win the newly-formed North Eastern Premier League.

From 1887 onwards, the then minor county Durham also used Ashbrooke as a base for entertaining the top international touring sides. The Australians played here on at least seven occasions between 1912 and 1977. In 1926 a crowd of over 22,000 packed into the ground for one of their games. Earlier and later games that took place in Sunderland were significant in the careers of the young Geoffrey Boycott, the young Sachin Tendulkar and the legendary Australian Spofforth. Ashbrooke also had a minor role to play in the great Australian Packer cricket controversy.

App1.1: Over 22,000 pack Ashbrooke to see the 1926 Australians

Hockey in the shape of Sunderland Hockey Club came to Ashbrooke a handful of seasons after the ground's opening. The sport has left Ashbrooke and then returned on a couple of occasions and today the hockey section uses the clubhouse as a central focus while playing on an artificial pitch elsewhere. On at least three occasions, full England international matches (for both male and female) were played at Ashbrooke and the hockey club has also provided players for the English national side.

App1.2: C T Green of Sunderland HC representing England in Edwardian times

Bowls arrived in 1889 in the shape of Sunderland BC. In the Edwardian period when a national bowling association was being set up, the club supplied internationals as well as one of the earliest winners of the individual national championship. The Ashbrooke Cup, played for since 1905, remains a prestigious regional competition.

App1.3: C Gibb of Sunderland BC - National Champion in the early 20th century

It is rather strange that tennis did not merit a verse in the bazaar song. Tennis as Sunderland LTC became part of the Sunderland Cricket and Football Club set-up shortly after the move to Ashbrooke in 1887 (although it was acknowledged in the 1890s that the sport was not at first massively popular). A club was already in existence before 1887 in nearby Thornhill Terrace and an 1886 membership booklet has survived in the Ashbrooke archives.

Still on the topic of tennis, Ashbrooke was, for many years, home to the prestigious Sunderland and Durham Championships. In the days before professional tennis, these were widely regarded as a good preparation for Wimbledon. The men's championship dates back to 1910. One of its finals, between New Zealander Malfroy and Mitic in the 1930s, appeared in a coaching manual of the 1950s, used as a copybook example of a tennis match. The ladies' championship, dating back to 1903, was won at one time or another by all three British Wimbledon champions - Ann Jones, Angela Mortimer and Virginia Wade. Wade's victory came in 1966.

Wider club spirit was high in the Edwardian period when the cricket, bowls and rugby were doing well and ladies' tennis in Sunderland was also very strong. This team revolved around the Aitcheson family and in particular around Helen Aitcheson who won Wimbledon titles and Olympic medals.

App1.4: Sunderland's successful ladies' tennis side outside the new pavilion

Squash did not come to Ashbrooke until the 1960s although there was an effort to incorporate the sport in the 1930s. Once in place, it took off as it did in many parts of the country causing an explosion in wider club membership. During the 1970s, there were six squash courts - all requiring significant notice for bookings. At the height of the squash boom in the late 1970s, the squash section had around 1,000 members. By the early 21st century the squash bubble had burst and a number of players had also moved elsewhere.

App1.5: Late 20th century squash at Ashbrooke

Although the Ashbrooke club has never had an athletics section per se, it was affiliated to the NCAA and athletics has always been part of the setup. The new ground was opened with an athletics meeting on May 30, 1887, and athletics was part of the 'healthy mind and body' package popular with the late Victorians. The Whitsuntide Sports, wonderfully recorded in a hand-written book in the archives, provided essential income for the wider club and these were eventually replaced by the popular annual Police Sports. The Police Sports ran, with a brief interval, until the late twentieth century and attracted large crowds. Olympic runners came to run in handicap races in the 1950s and the blood-curdling cycling race known as 'the devil take the hindmost' was much loved by youngsters. They positioned themselves so they could get a close up of the frantic riders coming off their bikes and hurtling along the cinder track which ran round the ground.

App1.6: Cyclists and a packed crowd in the 1950s

Occasionally school sports are still held at Ashbrooke, especially for the pupils at Argyle House School, and the clubhouse at Ashbrooke is used today as a base for Sunderland Strollers. This athletics club trains in the streets around the ground and grew up with the running boom created by Brendan Foster and his Great North Run in the 1980s. In the early twenty-first century, the club is strong both socially and competitively.

App1.7:
Sunderland
Strollers in race
action

Surprisingly there has been a football link too. A blue plaque marks the spot where Sunderland AFC played for one season in a field now forming part of the Ashbrooke ground. This was six years before the purchase of the field and neighbouring fields to be used for rugby and cricket. The occasional game of football has been played here since, especially in the early years of the twentieth century when officials of the wider club could find little use for a raised area on the western side of the ground. With the demise of grass field hockey, the hockey pitch has now become a football pitch used by the local university side. Members of the bar staff have also formed Ashbrooke FC, which hopes to play on the pitch soon. The team gained promotion in a local league during its first playing season. The floodlit tennis courts are also used for seven-a-side football on a regular basis and junior football coaching has also established itself on the ground.

Other sports played at Ashbrooke over the years include quoits, boules and baseball. The archive contains a folder full of material relating to a special baseball match held to celebrate the 1937 coronation of George VI. It was between a side from Yorkshire and the Canadian national team. The crowd was disappointingly small.

Relations Between the Rugby Section and Other Sports

The bonding of cricket and rugby came about in 1887 and was a natural one. Sunderland RFC had already used the cricket club's grounds at Holmeside and Chester Road before the move to Ashbrooke. Here the two clubs united as separate sections of the Sunderland Cricket and Football Club. Slightly later, Herbert Squance, a Sunderland cricketing rugby player, was a driving force behind the formation of the league in which the cricket team played.

In general, rugby and cricket managed to co-exist at Ashbrooke because their playing seasons did not clash. Despite this fact, a great deal of mutual tolerance and understanding has been necessary over the years. The rugby pitch lies on a great swathe of the outfield of the cricket pitch and has to be in reasonable shape for the cricket season. There has been some inevitable overlapping of seasons from time to time too necessitating discussion and give and take.

This has been the case throughout and a few problems faced in the 1950s provide good examples of the approach necessary. In the summer of 1956, the rugby club had to be careful about the timing of its youngsters' summer school as Durham and South Africa were due to play a cricket match. During the following year, the cricket section allowed the rugby posts to remain up longer than usual for a special match. A little later the cricketers agreed to reverse a fixture so that a touring Keswick side could play rugby at Ashbrooke. Durham Senior League officials, however, reversed the decision. The rugby section was thus forced to play the game on a council ground north of the river despite the generous offer from the cricketers.

Mumbling and grumbling across the two sports is inevitable. The rugby players would welcome another pitch or two across the cricket wicket and southern outfield while cricketers fielding to the north of the wicket frequently complain of the vagaries of bounce. All in all there are few on either side keen to end what has been a lengthy and generally amicable relationship. As late as 1989, the two sections of the club were playing each other at cricket with the rugby side coming out on top, thanks to a well-worked 50 by a member of the Boyd family.

Grass hockey died out gradually towards the end of the twentieth century but for many years hockey was played on the southern outfield of the cricket pitch. Problems were often created by a lack of changing space which could satisfy both rugby and hockey and at one point a newly introduced hockey whistle was so similar to the rugby one that it caused havoc in the oval ball game played on the neighbouring pitch. Despite this there seems to have been the same element of give and take as existed and still exists between rugby and cricket and when international hockey games came to Ashbrooke, rugby gave way in terms of fixtures and changing facilities. On one of these occasions, at least, a huge temporary stand was placed across the rugby pitch to accommodate spectators. The wider club's gain in terms of finance and kudos probably made the upset easier to bear.

Bowls is played in a corner tucked away at the opposite end of the ground to the rugby pitch and the bowls section has its own pavilion so is capable of leading a slightly separate existence from the main club. Being a summer sport, it has clashed little with rugby and this section of the wider club has probably benefited more from rugby over the years than vice versa. As will be seen in Appendix

Three, many a retired rugby player has used his eye for a ball to succeed on the bowling green in later life.

Tennis and rugby have also cohabited amicably at Ashbrooke. The courts have always been away from the rugby pitch and the big grass court competitions were played in summer on what was the hockey pitch in winter. On a number of occasions over the years, the rugby section helped out with stewarding and marshalling big events and rugby benefitted financially from the wider club's involvement in big regional show games played away from Ashbrooke in the mid 1950s.

In terms of athletics, the founding members of the Sunderland Strollers in the 1980s were mostly rugby players or ex-players. Squash, however, which caused a huge increase in wider club membership, brought mild panic to the rugby section. At a rugby committee meeting in the 1970s, one committee member suggested that it would be wise to "keep an eye" on squash lest it took over the entire club as it had done at Hull. Rugby players played squash for fun and competitively and the rugby section allowed the lady squash players to use their changing rooms during the week.

Such co-operation and amicability may seem rather strange but it goes a long way towards explaining why the wider club has survived. In the 1970s and 1980s, the rugby club AGM's were still closing with a vote of thanks to the other sections of the club for their helpfulness, tolerance, "assistance and willing co-operation".

Running the Wider Sports Club

As representatives of the rugby section of the wider sports club, the committee whose minutes have featured so heavily in the main story, formed a lower tier of the sports' club's organisation. This is a fact of some importance. From 1887 onwards, Sunderland Cricket and Football Club was under the control of a governing board and a set of trustees. In the pyramid of organisation, they stood above the sectional or individual sporting club committees that would, in the more common environment of a single sporting club, have been the sole decision-makers. Under such circumstances it is easy to see why the wider club was essentially conservative and why, at times, it is difficult to work out exactly who was doing what and why.

As a founding section of the wider club, rugby was represented on the governing board from the outset and had members as trustees and serving as wider club presidents over the years. When Ashbrooke was first set up, four rugby men were on the governing board and seven were serving as trustees.

Without going into too much detail, it is possible to catch a sense of the relationship between governing board and section from time to time. At one point in the 1920s it would seem that the governing board had a big say as to who served on the rugby club committee. In the early 1950s the rugby section Byelaws had to gain governing board approval, as did emergency expenditure on shirts. Such activities seem fairly typical over a long period of the wider sporting club's existence. By understanding the nature of this wider organisation, it becomes easier to appreciate some of the problems that arose across the rugby club's history. There were many such difficulties but these singled out below should help to complete the story.

The Search for a Social Life

In the years before the Second World War, the sports club at the Ashbrooke ground offered little to members in the way of social life after games. After the war, this became an issue for the rugby section. There was no buffet and no bar and none of the club atmosphere found at most other rugby clubs. Social drinking was done at the Palatine Hotel and 'The Vic' (Victoria Gardens public house) and some rugby committee members maintained that it dissuaded both players and opposition from becoming involved with the rugby club.

During the early 1950s there was a battle to get a licence and a bar and to provide social facilities especially for the younger players that the rugby club was keen on retaining. There were "lengthy wrangles" between the rugby section and the governing board over the issue with the rugby committee arguing that it was a duty to entertain visiting sides and that a bar would provide much needed revenue. In the 1950s a vote among the general membership turned down the idea and it was only when the rugby section began to talk about building a separate clubhouse that serious negotiations took place. The governing board wanted any change to take place within the current building as a separate clubhouse would divide the wider club. Representatives were sent out to see how other clubs ran their bars and since the 1956/7 season there has been a bar and a permanent licence and some form of stewardship.

Wider Club Membership

The complex nature of membership also added an extra tier of administration. All sports players were members of the wider club and as such were able to play their individual sports. This caused a problem when it came to attracting rugby players and in particular youngsters. At one point in the 1950s it was noted in the rugby minutes that people living on the cusp between the Sunderland club and another rugby club were likely to go to the other because of the membership costs. This point was made once again in the minutes of the 1970s.

Junior membership has always been a particular issue and this can be seen at its clearest in the 1950s. Keen to recruit more youngsters, the rugby committee began to subsidise junior membership by taking a flat fee from players and making up individual membership. At one point it was suggested that the section paid junior membership as a lump sum but the governing board turned this down. All sports players were to remain first and foremost individual members of the wider club and anything else would be setting a precedent. The issue of subsidising colts' membership was still around in the 1970s with membership of the wider club costing over £3 a year and the rugby section only charging £1 and then making up the shortfall.

Over the years, attitudes to this form of membership have changed. The Ashbrooke club now has both playing and social memberships with a junior membership linked to social use of facilities by parents.

Pitches

The question of playing pitches was an awkward one. Who, for example, should pay off the loan for the pitches at Ryhope Road purchased after the war? Only the rugby section and, on occasions, the hockey section, made use of them. The matter was raised on a number of occasions in various committees and never fully resolved. At times the rugby section seemed to be raising appropriate funds and at other times it was the wider club that bore the brunt of the cost.

Nor was the main rugby pitch at Ashbrooke sacrosanct and one related incident in the mid-1950s helps us understand more about the rugby club's history and its relations with the wider club. With Ashbrooke in financial crisis and needing money for capital development on the ground and surrounds, Sunderland AFC came in with an offer to rent the rugby pitch for a twenty-year period. The soccer club was in need of an enclosed pitch on which to play certain 'junior' matches and was able to offer space elsewhere to be used for two rugby pitches The resultant discussions that took place at the club's governing board level were full of interest. This was a tempting offer as much-needed money would be on the table and the rugby section would have more than the single pitch it had at the time. In the end the offer was rejected - battered down by a series of arguments. "Do we want professionalism at Ashbrooke?" the club president argued at one meeting while another board member noted that acceptance would spell "the end of Sunderland Cricket and Football Club". The nearest the rugby club would now be playing would be at Grangetown to the south or at Grindon to the west. 'Birthright' and 'tradition' were two other words used - and that proved to be the end of the matter.

Finance

As the question of renting the rugby pitch to the professional soccer club suggests, one of the main issues at Ashbrooke has always been money. In this respect, the complexity of Sunderland Rugby Club's finances can only be appreciated when they are set against the finances of the wider club - a club that catered for between 1,000 and 2,000 paid up members for most of the twentieth century.

The financial records in the archives are fairly full and will probably need a PhD student of sport administration to study them and sort them out. For the time being, a brief and hopefully simple outline should be enough to complete the story of Sunderland RFC.

The wider club was 'in hock' from the minute it moved to Ashbrooke in 1887. It had to find £11,500 to buy the various fields needed and did it with a £7,000 mortgage and the rest through gifts and debentures. It also had to help financially towards the construction of public roads around the ground.

The debentures (time-sensitive and bond-based personal loans which paid occasional dividends and/or interest) were guaranteed by trustees. In the 1920s, Lorry Squance decided funds were needed immediately and asked for further debentures guaranteed against the value of the ground (£10,000). These debentures were fully subscribed up to the £10,000 and due for repayment at 150% in 1952. It would seem that some debenture holders waived their 50% bonus while others waived their debentures completely when the end date arrived.

For many years (with occasional exceptions), the wider club barely survived, dependent on membership subscriptions, the proceeds of the Whitsuntide and other Sports, occasional gate money and ground lettings. The question of repaying long term debt was usually both out of sight and out of mind as the wider club lived from hand to mouth. After only seven years at Ashbrooke, the annual outlay stood at £1210 with income only £792. The wider club was running at a loss and also failing to pay off any long-term debt. The answer to this problem lay in the Grand Bazaar featured at the top of the chapter where Ashbrooke virtually took over the whole of the town for five days. The venture raised £2240. Just over £400 went to balance the books and the rest to the capital fund.

ASHBROOKE BAZAAR.

By W. PRIESTLY, Jun.

App1.9: Heading from Grand Bazaar song sheet, 1895

Despite this positive experience, the hand to mouth approach continued and in the Edwardian period; both the cricketers and the rugby players were asked to find for their own travel expenses. All this when the cost of membership had not been raised since 1860! When it was finally came to be raised in 1906 it was by almost 50%. This caused a great deal of consternation among the members. Senior membership went from a guinea or £1 and one shilling to £1 and ten shillings i.e. £1.05 to £1.50 - with junior membership half that.

The grand pavilion, still the club's pride and joy, opened in 1899 but there was no buffet or bar and little if any on-site socialising and that proved the case even after an extension in the 1930s. Around the same time, there was a fall in membership attributed in the governing board minutes to the "local state of trade". The Second World War made the position worse and, soon after, the wider club was again being run at an annual loss. Between 1947 and 1959 extraordinary expenses alone were estimated at £5,000 with special efforts over a decade or so only able to raise £4,500 as part cover. In light of this, the money gained by opening a buffet and securing of a licence in the 1950s was seen as a godsend.

Over the years individual members made efforts to raise money. H K S Marshall, brother of international rugby player Howard, ran a highly profitable sweep on the St Leger for a number of years assisted by his daughters. By the late 1970s, however, the old club was in serious need of capital investment and updating in order to compete with other organisations. Thus in 1979 Alan Bean, then club president, launched the Ashbrooke Foundation. This was put forward as "an opportunity to assist the club on a long-term basis". Members past and present "and other interested parties" were asked to subscribe to a fund, which could be used to finance the cost of major projects. Alan Bean expressed the hope that a capital fund of £250,000 could be built up over the following ten to fifteen years. In the 70s, this was a considerable amount

After an early hiccup, an appeal went out late in 1979 with a preliminary collection target set at £60,000 over the three years. Approximately half the targeted money came in at once and, in the following April, Dickie Jeeps, chairman of the Sports Council, visited the club to give encouragement (Jeeps had played at Ashbrooke in a final England rugby trial in the 1950s). By June 1980, the Ashbrooke Foundation had gathered in £34,000 in the form of donations, bankers' orders, pledges and legacies - mostly from former members. Considering the economic plight of Britain during the 'Winter of Discontent', this was quite an achievement. Some 200 donors were listed in the newsletter of the day although the author of the same newsletter did express some disappointment at the lack of interest shown by current members.

By the middle of 1981, eight trustees were running the Foundation and a sum of £14,500 had been released for immediate use. The first formal grant - £1,500 towards the computerisation of membership - came late in the following year. Donations now began to slow down although Alan Bean continued to stress the fact that the project was both long-term and ongoing. A generous donation of £12,000 from the estate of John MacMurray, a former Ashbrooke tennis player and cricketer, boosted the coffers and soon the sum ready for immediate use had risen to £29,000. Age was a problem too and the need to provide £4,000 to repair the water system illustrates the difficulty of keeping funds for entirely new projects. Alan Bean died in 1986 and for many years after, his watchful role was taken over by Robin Auld.

On reflection, it is now clear that the work of this foundation has been invaluable. However, sport was not tax-free so the capital fund was constantly being eaten away. The last remnants of the foundation's fund are still being used up today.

Unfortunately while this grand venture was being undertaken, general rising costs and declining membership had combined to make the day to day running of the club even more difficult. Like many other British heavy industrial centres in the 1980s, Sunderland was in recession as the mines and shipyards began to close. There was little money round, people were leaving the town and membership began to fall. In addition the old club was being challenged increasingly by new leisure centres/racquets clubs, and by nearby pubs attached to big chains. These had seemingly endless pockets for redevelopment even in time of recession. The newsletters of the early 1980s exude a real sense of depression, referring frequently to a crisis of "people and money". At times, there was an air of hopelessness as the club president anticipated turning over club and ground to housing, a supermarket chain or simply into the hands of the local council.

Since the 1980s, the raised area to the west of the ground has been sold for private housing and the Ashbrooke club has gained charitable status. Life continued to be difficult despite a valiant effort to celebrate the ground's centenary in 1987 and the introduction of various schemes to bring a more professional approach to the running of the wider club. As late as 2005, a note in a rugby club programme was still referring to "severe financial issues" and the necessity for the rugby section to pay its way.

Although it may be too early to judge, things seem to have been picking up over the last few years despite the recession of the early twenty-first century. In 2011 Ashbrooke is marketing itself as 'The Home of Sport in Sunderland' and boasting eight sporting sections (the traditional six, plus the Strollers and Broom Ladies' Hockey Club). Advertising refers to 'a comprehensive sports club with a modern state-of-the-art gym and a snooker room, a restaurant and facilities capable of coping with all sorts of functions from weddings and conferences to company fun days.

App1.10: Ashbrooke's modern marketing

More important still, finances seem to be under control with profits rising due to improved facilities and long-term debt problems being gradually solved. A real ale bar is tied to membership benefits and three big annual events - November 5th Fireworks, an early summer Beer Festival and the highly-rated Split Music Festival are targeted as major sources of income. Live music is also becoming part of the club's lifeblood thanks to the support of The Futureheads, an internationally known band whose first performance was at the club. Other well known bands such as Frankie and the Heartstrings, and Coal Train have membership links to Ashbrooke. Much of this progress has come under the astute presidency of Rob Deverson who joined the cricket section along with his young son towards the end of the twentieth century.

App1.11: Local bands help to save the day

Ashbrooke's modern image is an important one and key to survival as a reputation for being socially restrictive has clung to the wider club despite valiant efforts to ditch it. Curry refers to this reputation in his handwritten memoir composed just after the Second World War while many of the older citizens of Sunderland recall the 'members only' signs outside the pavilion from the days when they watched top class cricket and tennis there. In the early twenty-first century, there is no room for a restrictive approach and the club's charitable status relies on a stated aim to provide 'social interaction' and 'sport for all' in the city.

End Note

When the editors of English Heritage's invaluable *Played In Britain* visited Ashbrooke as part of preparation for the publication of the *Played in Tyne and Wear* volume, they were amazed at the survival of the wider sports club and its extensive archive. In fact the wider club was afforded its own chapter - a rare occurrence in these volumes. Perhaps the last words here should be given to the volume's editor

In the book itself, Lynn wrote of Ashbrooke...

> *"Once it was known as 'The Lord's of the North'. Today they call it 'the home of sport in Sunderland' - and rightly so."*

...and concluded the introduction to a chapter six pages (and thirteen photographs) in length thus:

> *"Here then is a special corner of Tyne and Wear, no longer the 'Lord's of the North' but a ground in a class of its own."*

App1.12: Ashbrooke's grand pavilion as it looks today

Appendix Two
Influential Ashbrooke - Some Essential Biographies

While material was being collected for this book, it became increasingly clear that a number of people associated with Sunderland RFC had left a considerable mark on the wider game of rugby. In a sense they have helped the club to 'battle above its weight' and have gained it a reputation somewhat larger than the one earned on the field of play. It was felt that their 'detailed inclusion' in the main body of the book there might have further complicated an already complex story so their personal stories are told here. The four men concerned are Eric Watt Moses, Alan Bean, Hartley Elliott and Robin Auld.

Eric Watt Moses (1895-1976)

Eric Watt Moses was a loyal Ashbrooke man all his life, and writers on the history of the game of rugby are in agreement that he had a considerable influence on the global progress of the game he loved. On his return to Sunderland from the First World War, during which he had served with distinction, he played for the club for a few seasons before turning to administration. He served as Honorary Secretary during the early 1920s while at the same time qualifying as a solicitor. During the same period, he was also involved in the running of the wider Ashbrooke club.

Later in the inter-war period, he turned his attention more and more towards county matters. His grounding as a young club secretary led to his undertaking the same role for Durham County for a number of years and also to serving as County President both before and after the Second World War. Meanwhile, as the county representative on the RFU, he began to make his mark at national and international level. He undertook this role from 1926 to 1950 and, during the same period, co-authored a detailed history of the first sixty years of Durham County rugby. His committee work was tireless at all levels and he seems to have revelled in it, serving on numerous committees and sub-committees of the RFU and often taking up senior positions on them. His interest in global rugby led him to the join the Dominions' Rugby and Home Unions Tours' committees and the International Board. He was also heavily involved in RFU finances and the organisation of the County Championship.

During the Second World War, he was an inspector in the Special Constabulary in Sunderland and in the years after it became clear to club members that he was destined for great things. In 1947 the Sunderland RFC committee, on which he still served, congratulated him on his appointment as Junior Vice President of the RFU. Natural progression led him to the post of Senior Vice President in the 1948/9 season and to that of President of the RFU for the 1949/50 season.

A great deal was going on in the world of rugby during the three years in which Eric Watt Moses was at his most influential although it would be naïve to suggest that he did it all alone or, indeed, was the main driving force behind all the measures. During this period the Australian RFU was established and the Southern Hemisphere international sides were placed on an equal footing with the home nations. The English Schools' RFU was also set up and the County Championship adapted.

The centenary history of the RFU published in the 1970s is also fulsome in its praise of his presidency. It was clear from the outset that he was a man on a mission keen to improve play on the field and to increase the global nature of the sport. He sent an inaugural message to every affiliated club in the world. An extract from this message gives some idea both of his passion and of his aims. Here he talks specifically about English rugby:

> "My principal memory of the past season is of the wide-spread enquiry 'what is wrong with English Rugby Football?', and even those two great victories over France and Scotland have not altered the fact that our game is passing through one of its periods of crisis. None of us can be happy or rest content with the present position, for the pre-war generation of players is finishing its gallant service, and their successors have picked up the game during the war years, and while it is all to easy to blame those years, war weariness and poor feeding, the fact remains that very many of our young players are all too ignorant of the fundamentals of the game.
>
> Our game can compete and more than hold its own with other Winter games if it is played properly and I therefore urge all the Constituent Bodies and Clubs to lay plans for an intensification of the early training so that players (including particularly the youngsters that join in club activities)... may be encouraged to think for themselves, to develop their own abilities and to become attack-minded."

His search for improvement in English rugby led him to accompany the British Lions on their tour of New Zealand. He returned from there convinced that the New Zealanders had "got it right" and that the Home Nations needed to make "a closer study of the game". Why he deserves his own section in this book should now be clear. Not only did he recommend this to all and sundry involved in the game, he returned to his home club after leaving the RFU presidency, took the club chair for three years, and 'put his money where his mouth was' at grass roots level (see Chapter Four). Only appointment to the chair/presidency of the Home Unions Touring Committee in 1953 brought this intense club stint to an end.

His work at national and international level continued apace. He became an RFU trustee and in the early to mid-1960s worked on re-framing the Byelaws of the game. The ensuing publication was regarded as a masterpiece at the time and he also wrote up the story of RFU administration during the years of his involvement to act as a helpmeet for other administrators. His history of the International Rugby Board from its formation in the late Victorian period was also well received and in the 1970s, one writer on the sport dubbed him 'The Scribe of the RFU' - an honour indeed.

App2.1: Eric Watt Moses

But the aim here is not simply to praise a local lad 'done good'. It is also to note his unstinting loyalty to the club overlooked by his native house. In later life his home was in Park Place West - a street associated with significant club members from the very early days. After the war, his professional duties were linked to the Sunderland Savings Bank and until his death, he devoted much of his time to the organisation and indeed very survival of the wider Ashbrooke Club.

In summary, the RFU's observation that Eric Watt Moses made 'a distinguished contribution to the development of the game' seems rather mild and does not quite paint the whole picture. During his presidency rugby was massively popular and a record crowd of 75,500 watched the England /Wales match of that season at Twickenham. The mark of the man is that on his departure from the club chair in 1953 he was made an honorary life member of the committee and also asked to see if he could persuade Wearmouth Football Club to loan the rugby club a spare pitch. Apparently the 2nd XV had nowhere to play on the following Saturday. In typical fashion, he successfully followed up the request.

Alan Bean (1902-1986)

Alan Bean was another dedicated Ashbrooke man with a massive enthusiasm for life and sport in various forms. In many ways his influence and success rival those of his long time compatriot Eric Watt Moses although their interests lay in slightly different areas of the sport of rugby.

As far as Sunderland RFC was concerned, Alan Bean gave invaluable service as both honorary secretary and as fixtures' secretary, jobs he carried out from his youth. He was also county representative and it is clear from the club minutes that he was a man who got things done even at a time when he was playing the game and organising tours. This was the case from his return to the club after study at Cambridge during the early 1920s. Like Eric Watt Moses, he also served on the wider club's governing board

At a higher level, Alan Bean's main claim to rugby fame came in the field of refereeing. He took this up in 1926 and rose rapidly in the ranks to be in charge of county games, international trials and, eventually, internationals themselves. He also refereed the Oxford v Cambridge 'varsity' match twice and the first ever match between the Barbarians and Australia.

Off the field, his influence was even greater as he made a considerable contribution to the improvement of refereeing standards. In the years after the Second World War, he was behind numerous successful refereeing courses held at Ashbrooke, Bisham Abbey and Hatfield College, Durham. Above all, he wrote the RFU bestseller *The Art of Refereeing*, which was greeted with great acclaim. His feat in producing the work was acknowledged in the club minutes.

App 2.2: Alan Bean

His endearing approach to the game he loved enabled him to communicate his passion to all that came across him. This approach can be seen in a brief extract from *The Art of Refereeing*:

"Rugby Football is a recreation played for the enjoyment primarily of the players. It follows that the referee's approach to his job must be positive and co-operative…. Rugby players are not criminals out to transgress the Laws. It is not an idle claim that Rugby footballers are in the main 'grand chaps' and grand chaps do not automatically become hardened cheats as soon as they step on a playing field."

The Ashbrooke club thus provided the 'scribe of referees' as well as that of more general rugby history.

Alan Bean was Senior Vice President and President of Durham County in the 1960s and a member of the important Mallaby Commission in the early 1970s. His interest in rugby and Sunderland RFC and rugby in general continued after this and well into the 1980s. Towards the end of his life he served for many years as president of the Ashbrooke Club and was a driving force behind the Ashbrooke Foundation.

In the 1970s revision of his book on refereeing (a revision in which Alan Bean was still involved) the new editor noted;

"This book is the work of Mr Alan Bean, who was a member of the International Panel of referees up to his retirement in 1950 and is the present chairman of the Referee Advisory Panel (1975)… Referees, and indeed all those players and spectators to whose pleasure they minister, should be eternally grateful to him."

Hartley Elliott (1908-2000)

Hartley Elliott was yet another who managed to keep club interests at heart while serving the sport of rugby at a higher level. His creation of the travelling Dolphins Rugby Club has already been dealt with in earlier chapters.

As a young man, he played rugby for Sunderland RFC around the time of some of the cup successes of the mid to late 1920s. Like his friend and mentor, Alan Bean, he entered the field of refereeing. Thanks to a younger friend, Robin Auld, his achievements as a referee and in other fields have been preserved in an archive, which now resides in the wider club archive. Numerous programmes and photographs tell of his success as a referee during the decade or so after the Second World War. He refereed the All Blacks, the Armed Forces, international trials and full internationals including games played in the Five Nations' Championship.

Much of his work was at county and national level and his daily work was based round the educational establishments in the City of Durham, leading to his heavy involvement in the running of sides connected with Durham University. Gerry Kirby, scrum half for the University 1st XV in the 1960s, remembers Hartley enthusiastically shouting advice and encouragement from the sidelines.

At county level, he served on numerous committees including coaching, schools, colts and selection and, as noted above, was particularly keen on encouraging schoolboy coaching. He served for eight years on the County Championship panel and in later life became a county trustee.

App2.3: Hartley Elliott, referee - Italy v France

It was due to his interest in improving the play of youngsters that Ashbrooke was gaining something of a national reputation for coaching in this period. From the early 1950s onwards, the much admired Durham County Union's Schoolboys'

Annual Rugby Coaching course was held at the ground. The course, aimed at not only coaching schoolboys but also at coaching coaches, was first held in 1950 and in generally recognised as the first of its type and groundbreaking in that it established the pattern for courses elsewhere. Serious organised coaching at senior level still lay in the future so here the idea was to bring together talented youngsters with players who had succeeded at international or trial level and to share their skills and experiences.

One of these players to attend was the young Carwyn James who later coached the 1971 Lions. Future internationals and Lions players such as Mike Weston (Durham City) and Johnny Dee (Hartlepool Rovers) were among those who benefited as schoolboys. Durham County was particularly strong on schoolboy rugby at this time with its county history of the mid-1970s claiming that it have more affiliated schools than any other county in the country. In September 1959, a group of 30 Danish players keen on promoting the game attended the course. In 1962 the course was extended to include players in the 16-21 age group.

Although younger than Alan Bean, Hartley Elliott worked with him closely in developing the referee courses, which were held at various venues in the 1950s. He was also England's representative on the International Panel of Referees for a number of years, taking over Alan Bean's mantle. The influence on refereeing of both Bean and Elliott can be gleaned from a couple of lengthy national newspaper reports in the Ashbrooke Archives. The rugby correspondent from the then *Manchester Guardian* attended one of the Durham Field Instructional Courses at Ashbrooke in the mid-1950s and wrote on it in glowing terms. He admired the course's simplicity, its aim being "to show a referee how to referee by showing him". He was also thrilled by the organisation and use of the "four referee instructors, eight referees and 35 players assembled by the Sunderland Club". "Most impressive and encouraging," he wrote and returned home after the course with a renewed faith in human will and nature. Many of the volunteer players were from Old Bedans and the annual course in 'Field Training' continued for a number of years, attracting referees from Liverpool and Cumberland along the way.

In 1960, Hartley wrote an article on Rugby Union for *Close Up*, the in-house magazine for the Armstrong-Whitworth Company. His interest in rugby as a sport for 'all classes' is clearly delineated here:

"It has often been said that Rugby Union football is a game for gentlemen of all classes, and there could hardly be a better definition of a game which, if it is to be played properly, demands a high standard of physical fitness together with a high degree of courage and skill. At one time it was a popular fallacy (possibly in view of the game's origin) that Rugby Union football was a game largely played by men educated at public schools, but this is (now) far removed from the truth. In every team and in every club, in all the rugby playing countries of the world, the greatness of the game is accentuated by the number of men from vastly different walks of life who mix and enjoy the tremendous spirit of companionship that is engendered."

Despite his numerous interests, Hartley remained essentially a club man and was still to be seen sitting quietly watching the games at Ashbrooke in the years just prior to his death. He was probably still acting as a referee assessor! One of his lasting legacies to the rugby club - and indeed the sports club in general - was his designing of the club badge, which came into use in the 1950s. Robin Auld captured the essence of the man in an obituary where he noted that this fierce 'amateur' was in a strange way extremely 'professional' in everything he did.

Robin Auld (b1926)

The emergence of Robin Auld as an administrator during the post was period is indicative of an Ashbrooke ethos or legacy in operation. Robin was (and still is) a fiercely proud Sunderland, Ashbrooke and rugby man although, ironically, it was association football that brought his family to the town. His grandfather Johnny Auld came from Scotland to play for Sunderland AFC and was part of the successful league winning sides of the 1890s. Johnny also played for his native country and made his international debut a couple of months before the opening of the Ashbrooke ground.

Robin Auld played rugby for the club and the county in the early 1950s although university and work took him off elsewhere (in the case of work –as a surveyor – to Africa where he wrote a much-admired report). He returned to Sunderland in the 1960s to teach at the Bede School where much was going on in the field of rugby both at school and at Old Boy level.

Robin was around at the time when Eric Watt Moses' pleas for improvement at all levels still held currency and he took these on board especially in the areas of coaching and schools rugby. Today it is almost a taken that organised coaching is part of the game. It was not ever thus. In most cases up to the Second World

War – and for a little time after – what coaching there was lay in the hands of the team captain and any committee member who was prepared to offer advice. If the improvement up to Southern Hemisphere standards was to take place there was a need for improved fitness and an increased awareness among players of team tactics and technical knowledge of the game.

App2.4 Robin Auld speaking at the centenary dinner

Organised adult coaching perhaps came out naturally from the schoolboy courses. During the late 1960s, Hartley Elliott had been involved in a coaching sub committee at county level. This committee built up relevant film and literature and offered help with coaching to individual clubs. Robin Auld served as secretary to this committee. In 1969, the county invited Don Rutherford, the newly appointed RFU technical adviser to a talk in and Robin attended the First

Annual Coaching conference on behalf of the county in the same year. He also spoke a Bisham Abbey on the subject of coaching.

By 1972 the sub committee and the coaching society had merged and had also begun regular meetings with the local referees' society. This created an effective hothouse of discussion with a number of Sunderland RFC officials involved including David Boyd, Harry Wilson and Ken Witherington. By the 1972/3 season Robin was Honorary Secretary of the Coaching Society, which had been established under the county wing. He was chairman of Sunderland RFC in its centenary season and president of Durham RFU in the mid 1980s. By then much of his work was involved with disciplinary procedures. In 1995 he produced a report for the county on the changing face of rugby. Dealing with communications, leagues, women's rugby and professionalism, the report of the Auld Commission was thorough and well received although, as Robin Auld himself admits, it was overtaken by events.

Robin continued to show an interest in the club into the twenty-first century and in particular continued his work with the Ashbrooke Foundation. In the centenary programme of 1973/4, he backed up friend Tony Greenwell's remark that 'Sunderland has never been a glamorous club but has been better known for the friendly atmosphere and determination to improve on and off the field'. A good note upon which to end this chapter.

Appendix Three
Sunderland RFC and the All-round Sportsman

Many of the sportsmen who played rugby for Sunderland RFC over the years have played other sports too - and frequently at a high level. They bring to mind the likes of C B Fry who excelled at a number of sports in the early twentieth century and Chris Balderstone who, later in the same century, managed to play professional football and professional cricket on the same day. This may or may not have been common practice elsewhere and may be an interesting topic for other local sports historians to follow up.

Summer Sports and Winter Sports

Some sports combined naturally and especially those which took place across different seasons. In this respect football (association and rugby) and cricket have been happy bedfellows across the years.

The link between cricket and rugby in Sunderland was always a firm one. Rugby started life on the town's cricket ground and proceeded to follow cricket around until the two clubs came together on a firmer footing in 1887 with the opening of the Ashbrooke ground and the formation of the Sunderland Cricket and Football Club. Under these circumstances, it was easy to move from one sport to the other.

Before the move to Ashbrooke, a number of cricketing rugby players had turned out for the two clubs at Holmeside and later at Chester Road. Francis Trewhitt and Harry (A H) Squance both played rugby in the club's first season by which time Harry had already featured in a Sunderland cricket side which had faced the travelling United South of England XI. During the summer of 1880, both men were in the XVIII of Sunderland cricket side, which played the touring Australians at Chester Road. Trewhitt is noted down as a rugby club official when Sunderland RFC won the first County Cup competition in 1881 and was also a member of the Durham County cricket XI from 1884-1888. Harry Squance's brother Herbert played rugby for Sunderland RFC and cricket for club and county in the 1890s. He was also the driving force behind the formation of cricket's Durham Senior League. There is also a photograph of county wicketkeeper James Chrisp in Sunderland RFC's 2nd XV in the late 1880s.

The Victorian and Edwardian periods brought a success to Sunderland and Durham cricket, equal to that enjoyed by club and county rugby - and there were a number of common threads. The most notable of these were the irrepressible rugby international Edgar 'Tegger' Elliot and Alleyne Burn (one of the sporting Burn brothers). Burn was older than Elliot by almost a decade. His rugby career stretched from the late 1880s to the late 1890s and his cricket career for the county from 1890 to 1906 with another three years' service to the Sunderland club thereafter. He played county rugby from 1890 to 1891. In his years as a county cricketer, he completed 67 innings and took 40 wickets (he was a slow bowler). His best batting season for the Sunderland club was in 1900 when he scored 533 at an average of 38.66, and in 1902 he took 72 wickets at a mere 7.70 runs per wicket.

'Tegger' Elliot was as much a star on the cricket pitch as he was on the rugby field. When Durham became a first-class county in 1993, cricket writer Jack Bannister described him as "one of the best batting talents" of his time and the man deserving of the 'best batting palm' for Durham County batsmen over the previous hundred years. In the 1930s, a county historian had already labelled him "the most brilliant batsman that ever played for Durham".

App3.1: 'Tegger' Elliot in Sunderland CC's 1st XI

Elliot's rugby career as a Sunderland, Durham, Barbarian and England player is dealt with elsewhere. His highest score with the bat was against Newcastle Garrison in 1905 when he made 332 runs in 225 minutes. For Sunderland CC and county he totalled 12,000 runs at an average well into the 30s. This includes a complete year lost to sport (1902), when he was serving 'with the horse' in South Africa. He also played for the Minor Counties and the Gentlemen of England. His two appearances for the 'Gentlemen' were rated as first-class appearances and gained him an entry in the massive *Who's Who of Cricketers*.

What is equally interesting is the number of occasions on which Elliot and Burn were on the same sports' field together. When Elliot began his rugby playing days at Ashbrooke, Burn was his captain for a couple of seasons (the Revd Wreford Brown, who was in the same rugby side, also played cricket for County Durham). Then there is a photograph of both Elliot and Burn in the Sunderland CC side that won the Durham Senior Cricket League in 1903. They played cricket together for Durham against a strong Lancashire side in the 1890s, South Africa in 1901 and the West Indies at Ashbrooke in 1906. Both batted well against South Africa while Elliot took 4-22 against the West Indies in seven overs. Elliot also made 53 against South Africa at Ashbrooke in 1907 before moving overseas.

Tegger's exiled brother, Harry, was as good a cricketer as he was a rugby player and during the year that he returned to England from working in the USA, he also played cricket with his brother at club and county level. In a county match against Northumberland in 1903, Harry Elliot scored 104 and Tegger 201. As in rugby, there were those who felt that Harry had greater potential as a player than his brother. Harry was also influential in running cricket in California.

Tegger Elliot had many admiring fans in and around Sunderland and they were prepared to tell a tale or two. On one occasion, while playing cricket for Sunderland at Durham City, he was barracked by some of the Durham City crowd. A couple of them decided to follow him to the railway station and continue the abuse. Elliot eventually tired of the pair, asked a friend to guard his bag and proceeded to sling both of them into a nearby ditch! He then picked up his bag and headed for the homeward train. When invited to appear in a first-class cricket fixture at the prestigious Scarborough Festival, he turned down the offer as he had already agreed to play for the club in a league game.

Family connections do not cease here. Two of the Pickersgill brothers - Charles and Edgar played rugby and cricket together at the club before the First World

War - often combining in the centres on the rugby field. Charles, an elegant left-handed batsman, completed ten innings for the county. Lorry Squance (E L) and his cousin Tom (T C) were both competent cricketers too. Lorry, one of those horribly talented sportsmen to whom everything came easily seems to have been 'laid back' and a great entertainer. His rugby success was achieved with little apparent effort while he played cricket for the club from 1909 to 1929 and for the county from 1912 to 1924 with a similar approach.

"Dapper, immaculately turned out, and always carrying a pervasive air of perfume about him, he was a man of many mannerisms and caps, who invariably turned on his way to the wicket to inspect the pavilion clock. Always sure of himself, he never weighed his chances austerely. The crowd got either their money's worth or he imperturbably retired for a blob." *(TAAB)*

App3.2: The dapper Lorry Squance

His 23 against Australia at Ashbrooke in 1921 was one of the few Durham batting successes of that game. His cousin, a club rugby player both before and after the First World War played cricket for Durham County in the 1920s. Both men were accountants and managed to dig the wider Ashbrooke club out of a financial hole on a number of occasions. The two Pickersgills and Lorry Squance were part of the cricket club's league winning side of 1911.

Had space allowed, it would have been possible to dedicate a full book to those Ashbrooke men who were adept at these two sports. Both Alan Bean and Hartley Elliott were keen cricketers and organisers of cricketing tours. There are photographs of some of those tours in the archives. Donald Greig gave years of service to the cricket club, captaining successful sides in the 1920s and 1930s. Clayton Greene, A C Dixon and Jenneson Taylor were also heavily involved in both sports. Jenneson Taylor brought a cricket team packed with top England players to Ashbrooke in 1930s. This was to celebrate the opening of an extension to the pavilion he had paid for in memory of his mother. In one league match against Whitburn in 1926, county rugby player Clayton Greene scored 128 not out and Lorry Squance 111…

Later in the century, Fred Wescott made a considerable contribution to both rugby and cricket at club level. Not only was he heavily involved in the administration of the wider club, he also captained the rugby 1st XV just after the Second War and a highly successful cricket 1st XI in the 1950s. There is an excellent photograph of this cricket side, which included two former England cricketers - the club pro, Alec Coxon, and Norman Mitchell-Innes both of whom had made a single appearance for their country.

In the 1960s and 1970s, Chris Storey and Frank Greenshields played both sports at a high level. Storey, fly half for club and county and much missed when working out of town, returned 8-55 playing for the county against Staffordshire and 6-23 against Cumberland in the 1970s. Greenshields succeeded for the county with both bat and ball against first-class opposition around the same time. As a junior, he opened the innings for the county with the legendary Colin Milburn. In the 1990s Chris and Frank came together to coach a highly successful Sunderland RFC junior rugby side which won County Cups and contained future England schools' and youth players (see Chapter Five). Keith Turnbull and Nick Hooper were two others who succeeded in both sports.

David Bains, currently playing in the backs for Sunderland RFC 1st XV, is a PE teacher at a large secondary school. He came up through the club's junior rugby ranks and represented the county at under 20 level. He played some cricket at Sunderland CC but now turns out for nearby Ryhope where he is a bowler who has recorded a league century as a batsman. David says that he rarely comes across current rugby players while playing cricket.

Rugby and outdoor athletics would also seem to combine well - the one a winter sport and the other followed up in the summer. The flying winger might fancy his chances at the 100 yards or 100 metres while some forwards have shown prowess in field events such as the hammer or the javelin.

The Ashbrooke club has never had an official athletics section as such although the Sunderland Strollers are now advertised as part of the wider sporting club. In the nineteenth century, the Bank Holidays Act made possible the annual Whitsuntide Sports in Sunderland - as it did in many major towns and cities. This event was a good fundraiser and a golden opportunity for the rugby players to show their prowess. In 1875, two of the Kayll brothers competed against each other in the mile race. In the following year and in front of a crowd of 7,000 at Chester Road, John Fowles and Francis Trewhitt (then aged 19) were among the competitors in the Sports. Trewhitt later served on the committee that organised the sports, as did rugby club founder Arthur Laing and two of the club's rugby internationals Tegger Elliot and Norman Cox. William Bell, who once played rugby against the touring Maoris, acted as lap recorder for a number of years.

In the 1870s and 80s, Sunderland RFC was also able to boast a star of early field athletics. Henry Kayll, the club's first international, was an expert pole-vaulter during the period in which wooden poles were used (up to the 1890s this was the case; thereafter they were made from bamboo for a while). A German athlete made the first noted record jump for the pole vault in 1789. From 1839, the British dominated the sport. In 1877 the record stood at just under 11 feet when Henry, (a "barrier breaker" according to one American web site), topped the mark by three-quarters of an inch. This remained a record for ten years when it was beaten by an American pole-vaulter. The Americans dominated pole vaulting in the twentieth century and the record now stands at well over twenty feet.

By the 1890s, the Whitsuntide Sports were a fixture at Ashbrooke and an invaluable hand-written book from the time logs events from 1893 to 1910. This book is now in the Ashbrooke archives and lists the names of all the competitors and in some cases their addresses too. Tom Crow, acknowledged in *TAAB* to have been a fine athlete as well as a good rugby player, entered the 100 and 220 yards in 1893. He was off a very low handicap - a sign of his ability. His brother also ran over the short distances. Moffet, Moore and Pinkney were other athletes whose names turned up in club sides at that time - also Leonard Iliff who featured on a 2nd XV photograph from the mid-1880s; he was a competitor in the one-mile bicycle race and lived a few yards away from the club's main entrance.

As noted previously, running came into vogue again in the early 1980s with the advent of the Great North Run. Rugby players David Boyes and Graham Young were active in the formation of the Sunderland Strollers which is chiefly a road running club.

A number of past players combined competitive tennis and rugby although generally few in number and early in the history of both clubs. Competitions held by the tennis club prior to the move to Ashbrooke featured familiar names such as Francis Trewhitt, J J Kayll, A G Hudson, A H Squance and England rugby international Charles Elliot. By the 1890s, W H Bell who was to have his fingers in many sporting pies was carrying off the tennis club's Hartley Cup. Harry Squance won the same trophy on two occasions and both Squance and Bell were involved in the early days of county tennis.

App3.3: W H Bell (dark jacket) and Learie Constantine (front left) on the same picture

By 1906, when the Ashbrooke ladies' tennis team was winning the national championship, another familiar name appeared on the tennis horizon - Tegger Elliot. In that year he won the men's club championship. This competition included as a guest, Australian cricketer and Davis Cup player Les Poidevin who had come to England to study medicine and had stayed. He was part of a successful Lancashire cricket side. Charles Pickersgill was also an enthusiastic tennis (and squash) player and represented the county. There are a number of photographs of him playing in and organising club championships in the 1920s. Few players have linked the two sports at the wider club in recent years.

The move from rugby to bowls also seemed a natural one. Bowls has always had the reputation as a game for those advanced in years, which is a pity as youngsters tend to advance rapidly in the sport when they take it up. With a proven eye for a ball, former rugby players quickly adapted to the sport and the mid-twentieth century provides us with two good examples of this. Charles Pickersgill, who had already played a number of sports at a high level, became a member of a successful Ashbrooke four-man rink in the 1930s. This rink won a couple of national titles and its members were All England rink champions in 1935 and News Chronicle Gold Cup All England Champions in 1936. In 1955, Pickersgill became chairman of the bowls section. Some thirty years earlier he had been President of Durham County RFU at the time of the successful All Blacks' visit to Sunderland. Donald Greig played his bowls at Ashbrooke twenty years later. When he was appointed chair of bowls in 1963, he completed a hat trick as he already chaired both rugby and cricket sections in times past.

App3.4: Cartoon of the multi-talented Charles Pickersgill

Today there are few bowls players who played rugby at the club when younger. A C 'Chappie' Harrison was full back for the 2nd XV in the 1959 cup-winning side and captain of the successful 3rd XV of 1961. He continued to give the rugby club long and invaluable service on and off the pitch and does the same for the bowls section half a century later.

Rugby and Other Winter Sports

The clash between rugby and other winter sports would seem to make it difficult for individuals to compete in more than one of these sports yet this was not always the case. The Squance family was involved in hockey in the sport's early days. Herbert Squance started off by playing rugby but then moved on to help to form the club's hockey team. He was also behind the formation of the Durham County hockey team and captained it in 1893. Later, Lorry Squance, a talented rugby-cricketer, played for the hockey 1st XI on a number of occasions. Frank Pickersgill also dabbled with rugby before embarking on a remarkable hockey career which began in the Victorian period and stretched well into the twentieth century. While playing his club hockey at Ashbrooke, he made 120 appearances for Durham County, captained the North of England side and came close to international honours. During the summers he appeared for Sunderland's cricket 1st XI alongside his two rugby-playing brothers Charles and Edgar. Charles Burn, whom we have to thank for many of the early photographs in the archives, also played both hockey and rugby. A keen sportsman from a sporting family, he arranged a game of cricket between his sporting friends and relations and their 'ladies' in 1907 - an event beautifully captured in one of his photographs.

App3.5: A photograph from Charles Burn's collection

Fred Wescott made 15 appearances for Durham County hockey XI after 1935 and represented the Ashbrooke club at the Bridlington Festival in 1949. A couple of years earlier he had captained rugby's 1st XV and he was later to captain a highly successful Sunderland CC 1st XI. There is also a photograph of Hartley Elliott in a hockey side at the Bridlington Festival.

App3.6: Hartley Elliott (back row with scarf)
at the Bridlington Festival

The least likely crossover was between rugby and association football. This certainly seems to have been the case in the 1880s when the lists of those who played both sports in the town reveals little cross-fertilisation, although one member of the Squance family did turn out for Sunderland AFC 2nd XI in the year they played at Ashbrooke. Unfortunately as was the practice at the time, the newspaper report failed to provide him with an initial and as there were many young sports-playing Squances around at the time, the name of the soccer player remains unknown. The remarkable Charles Pickersgill managed to find time to make a number of amateur appearances for Sunderland AFC in the early twentieth century.

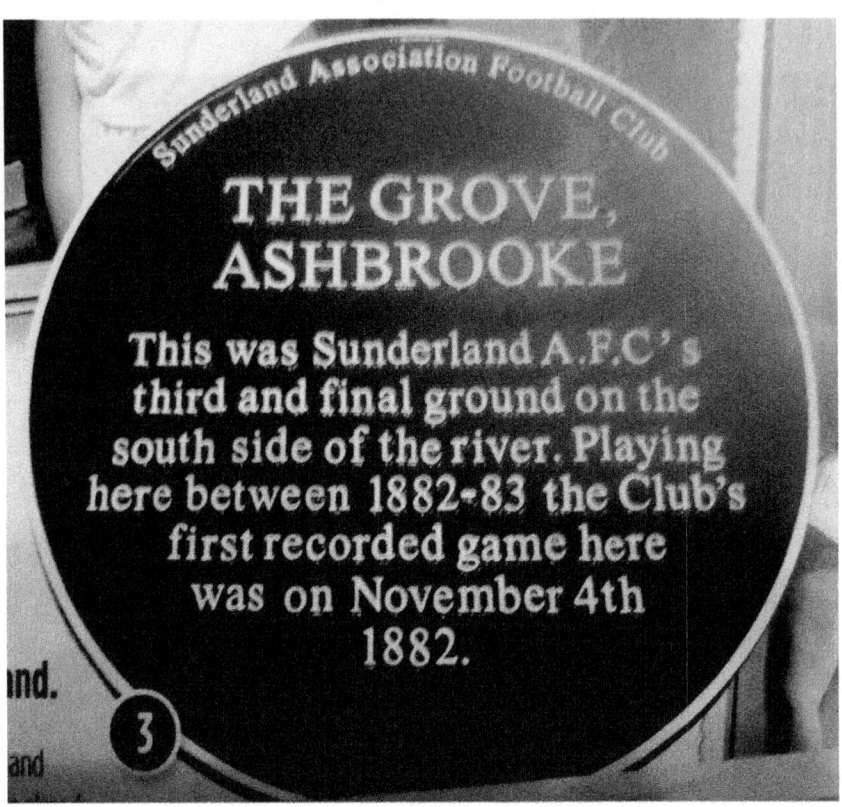

App3.7: A reminder of Sunderland AFC's links with Ashbrooke

Rugby and Squash (and the rest)

As an all-year round and indoor sport available at Ashbrooke for the last fifty years, squash is perhaps a special case and has attracted a number of rugby players to it. A rugby player - Charles W Pickersgill - started the section in the early 1960s. He had captained one of the rugby club's most successful sides, the 2nd XV of 1948/9 that lost only six games all season and recorded 619 points for and 126 against. He was also the first chairman of the squash section. Towards the end of the twentieth century, Sunderland rode high in the northern squash world and significant rugby players such as Chris Storey and Charlie Bentley were among those who brought about this success. Charlie Bentley still plays today.

App3.8: The multi-talented Chris Storey in a regional squash competition

As to other sports, it is recorded that Victorian rugby international Francis Poole was an excellent water polo player and represented Oxford University while Alleyne Burn was a skilled oarsman. In more recent times, 1st XV back John Gregson played American Football for Leeds Celtics alongside his brother Paul, who also appeared in the front row for the 1st XV. Paul also represented Great Britain Bulldogs at American Football and later turned his attentions to semi-professional mixed martial arts.

Some Special Cases and Conclusions

From the information gathered above, it is not difficult to conclude that some remarkable all-round sportsmen have appeared in the colours of Sunderland RFC over the years. From this impressive list, Francis Trewhitt, numerous members of the Squance family, Alleyne Burn, Tegger Elliot and his brother Harry, Charles Pickersgill and, more recently, Fred Wescott and Chris Storey stand out. They all played a number of sports at a high level. In the case of those playing in the early years of the club's existence in particular, it could be argued that their lifestyles afforded them the time to do this. Many were in charge of their own destinies when it came to organising work time - a position enjoyed by few.

App3.9: Fred Westcott - hockey-playing captain of rugby and cricket first teams

An initial examination of the state of play today would suggest that the days of the all round sportsman have gone. The high demands of individual sports may be given as a reason for this as well as the extension of the season at both ends in the case of sports such as football, cricket and rugby. However, there is at least one exception. The movement of some amateur rugby league fixtures to the summer months has opened the door for union players prepared to put their battered bodies on the line the whole year round. In recent years a number of club players including Ed Bengochea, Tom Hirst, Peter Harrison and Peter Carter have found time for both rugby codes.

A Short Bibliography

The main source for the book has been the Ashbrooke archives which have been collected and collated over the last few years, and are in the process of being housed in a room at Ashbrooke. The archives used include the minutes of the rugby club and the wider club's governing board; newsletters; photographs and personal archives placed in the wider archive. These are referred to in the text. The archives are being indexed and there is already a schools' project to help youngsters to a wider understanding of the nature of historical research.

In addition to the Ashbrooke archive material, the following books have been consulted:

Casey, Patrick and Hale, Richard I, 2009, For College, Club and Country – A History of Clifton Rugby Football Club, MX Publishing

Owen, O. L., 1955, The History of the Rugby Football Union, Playfair Books Ltd

Titley, U.A. and McWhirter, Ross, 1970, Centenary History of the Rugby Football Union, Rugby Football Union

Huggins, Mike, 2004, The Victorians and Sport, Hambledon and London

Norridge, Julian, 2008, Can We Have Our Balls Back Please? How the British invented Sport, Penguin

Ellis, F (Ed), 1975, The Art of Refereeing -A Handbook for Rugby Union Referees, Rugby Football Union

Anon, 1939, London Society of Rugby Football Referees Jubilee History 1889 to 1939, Blackheath Press

Watt Moses, Eric (collator), 1963, To Ashbrooke and Beyond 1808 –1963, Sunderland Cricket and Football Club

Berkeley Cowell, C and Watt Moses, E, 1936, Durham County Rugby Union – Sixty Year Records of the County XV (1876 –1936), Durham County RFU

Scott, W.J.R (Ed), 1976, Durham County Rugby Union – Records of the County XV (1936 –1976), Durham County RFU

Marshall, Howard, 1951, Oxford v Cambridge, The Story of the University Rugby Match, Clerke and Cockeran

Elders, John (Ed), 1977, Royal Grammar School Newcastle Upon Tyne Rugby Football Club 1877 –1977. RGS Newcastle

Bannister, Jack and Graveney, David, 1993, Durham C.C.C. Past, Present and Future, Queen Anne Press

Bell, Wm R, 1931, Fifty Years History of the Durham County Cricket Club 1882 – 1931, Durham C.C.C.

Fox, Dave; Bogle, Ken and Hoskins, Mark, 2006, A Century of the All Blacks in Britain and Ireland, Tempus

Also other primary sources

Handbook of the Grand Bazaar in aid of the Sunderland Cricket and Football Club, November 1895 (author's collection)

Curry, R, 1948, Sunderland Cricket and Rugby and Rugby Football Club 1890 to 1948, unpublished hand written Sunderland Local Studies Library

Donald Greig's 1920s scrapbook (John Buddington collection)

And useful web sites

The Genealogist (subscription) and Family Search (free) are two excellent research web sites for family history and discovering details of people alive between 1837 and 1911 in particular.

http://www.thegenealogist.co.uk/   https://www.familysearch.org/

http://members.cox.net/ggthomp01/jameslaing1823.html

is excellent on the Laing family

Also from MXPublishing

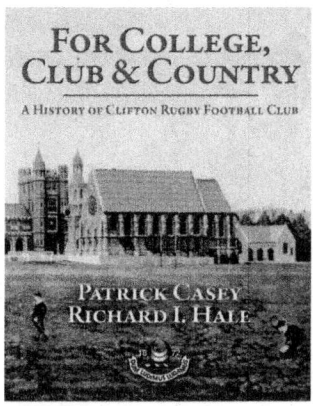

For College Club and Country - A History of Clifton Rugby Football Club

"Richly illustrated with team photographs over more than 100 years, this is a fascinating piece of social history based around one of the oldest rugby clubs in the country. Providing moving accounts of club members who lost their lives in the two World Wars, this is an important and fascinating history of a club that has retained a strong community focus"
The Bookbag

Rugby Football During the Nineteenth Century

"There have been some cracking rugby history books down the years, but never have we been treated to rugby writing by the men who were there at the time. Until now"
Rugby World Magazine

Lightning Source UK Ltd.
Milton Keynes UK
UKOW05f1445211217
314810UK00005B/189/P